MW00364626

12 MONTHS OF FUN!

THE LOBSTER KIDS' GUIDE
TO EXPLORING
SEATTLE

BY SHELLEY ARENAS
AND
CHERYL MURFIN BOND

Lobster Press™

Arenas, Shelley, 1958-
Murfin Bond, Cheryl, 1966-
The Lobster Kids' Guide to Exploring Seattle: 12 Months of Fun!
Text copyright © 2001 by Lobster Press™
Illustrations copyright © 2001 by Lobster Press™

All rights reserved. No part of this publication may be reproduced,
stored in any retrieval system or transmitted, in any form or by any
means, without the prior written permission of Lobster Press™.

Published by
Lobster Press™
1620 Sherbrooke St. W., Suites C & D
Montréal, Québec H3H 1C9
Tel. (514) 904-1100, Fax (514) 904-1101
www.lobsterpress.com

Publisher: Alison Fripp
Editor: Alison Fischer
Managing Editor: Bob Kirner
Copy Editor: Frances Purslow
Cover and Illustrations: Christine Battuz
Icons: Christiane Beauregard and Josée Masse
Layout and Design: Olivier Lasser

Distribution:
In the United States
Advanced Global Distribution Services
5880 Oberlin Drive, Suite 400
San Diego, CA 92121
Tel. (858) 457-2500
Fax (858) 812-6476

In Canada
Raincoast Books
9050 Shaughnessey Street
Vancouver, BC V6P 6E5
Tel. 1-800-663-5714
Fax 1-800-565-3770

We acknowledge the financial support of the Government of Canada
through the Book Publishing Industry Development Program (BPIDP)
for our publishing activities.

National Library of Canada Cataloguing in Publication Data

Murfin Bond, Cheryl, 1966-
The Lobster kids' guide to exploring seattle: 12 months of fun!

Includes index.
ISBN 1-894222-27-X

    1. Family recreation—Washington (State)—Seattle—Guidebooks.
2. Children—Travel—Washington (State)—Seattle—Guidebooks.
3. Amusements—Washington (State)—Seattle—Guidebooks. 4. Seattle
(Wash.)—Guidebooks. I. Arenas, Shelley, 1958- II. Battuz, Christine
III. Kirner, Bob, 1959- IV. Title.

F899.S43M87 2001   917.97'7720444   C2001-900046-4

Printed and bound in Canada

Table of Contents

Authors' Introduction

As writers and residents of Seattle, we thought we had experienced the city inside and out. Then we had kids, and not long after became editors at a local publisher of parenting periodicals. Suddenly the Seattle we thought we knew was bigger and a lot more fun—with an abundance of child-focused places to play, learn and explore. What a delight it has been to discover a city we might never have known as childless adults—one that offers families unlimited possibilities for adventure.

Writing this book has taught us that Seattle is a city of endless rediscovery. Every neighborhood boasts its own particular jewels and each attraction becomes doubly wondrous when experienced through the eyes of a child.

If your family is vacationing in Seattle, this guide will provide great ideas for exciting outings. If you live in the Emerald City, we encourage you to explore the many treasures just outside your door.

Deepest thanks Jeff, Madeleine, Aidan and Christy—wonderful partners in fun and companions in life. Special thanks to Stephanie, Sheila and Ron, and Sarah. I dedicate this book to Children's Home Society of Washington—for turning hope into reality for children and families for more than 100 years.

CHERYL MURFIN BOND

I dedicate this book to the two wonderful kids in my life—Dominic and Ashley, my Emerald City co-explorers. To my family, friends and the Center for Spiritual Living, I give my heartfelt appreciation. Thanks to Lobster Press™ for this chance to share my knowledge and love of Seattle.

SHELLEY ARENAS

A Word from the Publisher

Lobster Press™ published its first book, *The Lobster Kids' Guide to Exploring Montréal* in 1998. Since then, the Kids' City Explorers Series has grown and now includes guides to other major Canadian cities. Due to the resounding success of the Canadian series, this year Lobster Press™ is publishing books for families exploring cities in the United States.

Whether you're a tourist, resident, parent or teacher, this book is a complete resource of things to do and see with kids in the Seattle area. It's jam-packed with valuable, timesaving information and great ideas for outings.

Shelley Arenas, Cheryl Murfin Bond and their families visited the sites in this guide in 2000-2001. All information provided has been verified. However, since prices and business hours are subject to change, call ahead to avoid disappointment. Please accept our apologies in advance for any inconveniences you may encounter.

To get the most out of this guide, please familiarize yourself with our "Lobster Rating System" and table of icons. These features let you know what our authors' families thought of each site and what amenities are available. Please note that traveling distances to the sites were determined from Seattle Center.

If you have comments about this book, visit our website and complete our on-line survey. Let us know if we've missed your family's favorite destination, and we'll include it in the next edition!

One last word: Please be careful when you and your children visit the sites from the guide. Neither Lobster Press™ nor the authors can be held responsible for any accidents that might occur.

Enjoy! And watch for the other books in the Kids' City Explorer Series. Now available: Boston, Chicago, Las Vegas and San Francisco. Coming in 2002: Halifax, Miami, New Orleans, Québec City and San Diego.

FROM THE GANG AT LOBSTER PRESS™

The Lobster Rating System

We thought it would be helpful if you knew what Shelley Arenas, Cheryl Murfin Bond and their families thought about the sites in this book before you head off to visit them. They rated every attraction and activity they visited for its:

☞ enjoyment level for children
☞ learning opportunities for children
☞ accessibility from Seattle Center
☞ costs and value for the money

A one-lobster rating: Good attraction.

A two-lobster rating: Very good attraction.

A three-lobster rating: Excellent attraction.

Not fitting some of the criteria, and subsequently not rated, are green spaces, festivals and various similar, nearby or other attractions.

Table of Icons

These facilities and/or activities are represented by the following icons:

Beach		Parking	
Bicycling		Picnic tables	
Birthday parties		Playground	
Bus stop		Restaurant/ snack bar	
Cross-country skiing		Restrooms	
Downhill skiing		Skating	
First aid		Snowshoeing	
Hiking		Swimming	
Ice cream stand		Telephone	
In-line skating		Tobogganing	
Information center		Wheelchair/stroller accessible	
		Wildlife watching	

Metro Transit, serving metropolitan Seattle and surrounding King County, offers bus routes to many of the destinations mentioned in this book. Route numbers, times and bus stop locations, however, are subject to change. Unless otherwise noted, routes listed in "Getting There" depart from the downtown Seattle bus corridor, which extends north to Battery St., south to S. Jackson St., from 6th Ave. to the west and east to the Waterfront. This corridor is a Ride Free zone, where travelers ride free daily between 6 am and 7 pm. For specific route information, call the Rider Information Office at (206) 553-3000. Tell the customer service representative the address where you are and the address of your destination and he or she will provide bus route and schedule details. Visit Metro Transit online at http://transit.metrokc.gov for more information and to use the automated trip planning services.

CHAPTER 1

LOCAL ATTRACTIONS

Introduction

Seattle is the punch line for many a joke about rain. But take a ride to the top of the Space Needle on a sun-streaked afternoon following a shower and you'll see why it's also called the Emerald City. With snow-capped mountains framing the horizon, two shimmering bodies of water lapping at the city from all angles, myriad parks and open spaces, and tons of kid-friendly attractions, Seattle sparkles and shines for families.

Whatever the weather, it's easy to find fun, educational outings for the whole family. There are obvious places to start your tour of the city. Seattle Center is home to the Pacific Science Center and the Experience Music Project. These major attractions should not be missed even if your stay is short. Equally impressive and all within a half-hour's drive of Seattle Center are the world-famous Museum of Flight, Alki Beach, funky Fremont, Pike Place Market, the Hiram M. Chittenden Locks and massive Safeco Field.

Wherever you start your day, be sure to save time and mental energy for the traffic. Whether you're traveling by bus, car, bicycle or on foot, Seattle roads can be a challenge.

Where Liberty Reigns
ALKI BEACH AND COMMUNITY

**Located along Alki Ave. S.W. and Beach Dr. S.W. along
the seaboard and west to 61st Ave. S.W., Seattle
(206) 932-5685 (West Seattle Chamber of Commerce)**

Who needs New York? If you've dreamed of seeing the Statue of Liberty but have no plans to fly east, go to West Seattle instead. Think of West Seattle and Alki Beach as Seattle's Ellis Island, complete with its own Lady Liberty. The statue is a miniature replica of the French gift to New York. It was erected by the Seattle Boy Scouts in the 1950s and stands above a time capsule from that era.

Lady Liberty, on the beach in the 2700 block of Alki Avenue S.W., is one of the reasons to put Alki on your must-see list. Alki monument (63rd Ave. S.W. and Alki Ave. S.W.) is another. It was a gift to Arthur Denny, a city pioneer who first landed in 1851, from his daughter. It includes a piece of the actual rock where Denny landed. Along the way, check out Alki Point Lighthouse—it began operating in 1887 and is still working today. If you are in the mood for more history, head to Log House Museum (page 194). This near century-old log carriage house overflows with early Seattle history.

The best reason to visit Alki with kids is the beach. Stretching several miles along Alki Avenue and Beach

Drive S.W., Alki Beach offers everything a kid could want—sand, rocks, crashing waves, sand-sculpture competitions (call the number above for dates), in-line skate rentals, a riding and walking boardwalk, beach volleyball and other sports, fun monuments and food stops. There's even an official pirate landing. Each July, Seattle's belching, scowling, but family-friendly Seafair Pirates make their official debut at Alki (206-728-0123 for Pirate and Seafair Summer Festival information).

SEASONS AND TIMES
➤ Year-round: Daily. Lighthouse (Memorial Day—Labor Day): Sat—Sun; call for hours (206) 217-6124. Most businesses operate regular business hours.

COST
➤ Beach: Free. In-line skate rentals: Generally $5 per hour. Lighthouse tour: Free. Log House Museum: Suggested donation adults $2, children $1.

GETTING THERE
➤ By car, from Seattle Center, head east on Mercer St. to I-5 South. Take I-5 S. to the Spokane St./West Seattle Bridge Exit and head west. Take the Harbor Ave. Exit. Turn north onto Harbor and follow it until it turns into Alki Ave. S.W. About 20 minutes from Seattle Center.
➤ By public transit, take Metro bus 37 or 56 west from downtown Seattle. Call Metro Transit for route and schedule information (206) 553-3000.

NEARBY
➤ Lincoln Park, Alki Park and Playground, Fauntleroy ferry terminal and access to Vashon Island.

COMMENT

➤ Alki Beach can be chilly even on a hot day, so bring a sweater or windbreaker. Strollers, in-line skates, bicycles, and other recreation equipment welcome. Plan a 3-hour visit.

Hail to the Music Makers
EXPERIENCE MUSIC PROJECT

325 – 5th Ave. N., Seattle
(877) 367-5483 or (206) 770-2700
www.emplive.com

Tell the truth. Do you sometimes grab that air guitar and jam out your own version of "Louie, Louie?" Do you get wistful thinking about Janice Joplin or Jimi Hendrix and wish your kids knew about these rock icons? If you answered "yes" to these questions, the Experience Music Project (EMP) is the place for you. Paul Allen's $240 million shiny metallic blob monument to American rock is Seattle Center's newest spectacle and a must-visit for any true groupie. Even if you're not a rock'n' roll fan, it's worth a trip. There's no other museum of its kind in the world.

Kids and adults alike will get a kick and education out of the interactive exhibits. In the Sound Lab, high-tech gadgetry helps visitors learn to play keyboards, drums and other instruments in minutes. You can even take your gang into one of 12 "sound pods" to work on group vocals.

Nearby at the On Stage exhibit, visitors step into a soundproof stage to play back-up to the rock anthem "Wild Thing" before a simulated audience. The Artist's Journey provides a fun, amusement-style ride using computer-generated special effects and a motion platform to take the audience on a wild music and video journey. Don't miss the stories-high Sky Church music and video room—it's a feast for the senses.

Be prepared to explain the exhibits to kids under age seven—the digital self-tour machines are too heavy for them to carry.

SEASONS AND TIMES
➤ Summer (Memorial Day—Labor Day): Daily, 9 am—11 pm.
Winter (Labor Day—Memorial Day): Sun—Thu, 10 am—6 pm;
Fri—Sat, 10 am—11 pm.

COST
➤ Adults $19.95, students (13 to 17) $15.95, children (7 to 12) $14.95, under 6 free. Annual individual membership $45, annual family membership $100.

GETTING THERE
➤ By car, from I-5 take the Mercer St. Exit and head west towards the Space Needle. The EMP is located on 5th Ave. on the northeast side of Seattle Center. Some free parking is available on nearby streets. During special events, parking fees at Center lots are based on the number of people in the vehicle (discounts for 2 or more). Expect to pay from $6 to $12 for all-day parking.
➤ By public transit, more than a dozen Metro bus routes service Seattle Center. Call Metro Transit for route and schedule information (206) 553-3000. Or ride the Monorail that travels between Seattle Center and downtown Seattle's Westlake Center.

NEARBY

➤ Seattle Center, Space Needle, Children's Museum, Seattle Children's Theatre, downtown Seattle, Monorail, Pike Place Market, Waterfront, Queen Anne Hill.

COMMENT

➤ Expect crowds on weekends and throughout the summer. Baby changing stations available. Plan a 2- to 3-hour visit.

Fun and Funk in
FREMONT

Located along N. 34th, 35th and 36th streets between Evanston N. and Aurora avenues, Seattle (206) 547-7440 (Fremont Arts Council) www.seattleweb.com/cities/fremont/fremont.html

If your kids believe the world revolves around them, here's the chance to set them straight. Just beyond Fremont District's 53-foot rocket (Evanston Ave. N. and N. 35th St.) stands the official marker for the Center of the Known Universe. After gazing at this funny tourist attraction, pick up a walking tour guide from one of the nearby kiosks and embark on one of the funkiest tours around. Wander east on N. 36th Street for a glimpse of the giant Fremont Troll under Fremont Bridge. Several blocks to the west a statue of Vladimir Lenin stoically rules over what locals call "The Republic of Fremont."

Fremont is also home to Seattle's famous statue, *Waiting for the Interurban.* It's a popular place for marriage proposals, birthday greetings, birth announcements and more. The constant decorations, clothes and notes adorning the statue might be considered graffiti in some cities, but here it's all part of the fun.

A trip to Fremont would not be complete without a stop at Still Life in Fremont Coffeehouse, the area's popular health-conscious eatery. Take a post-meal stroll along the Ship Canal—it's quiet, stroller-friendly and picturesque. Kids love the dinosaur sculpture and working drawbridge on the way. Be sure to save time for a free tour of History House Museum (page 189). It's a great way to learn about Seattle neighborhoods. The Collectible Doll Company (4216 – 6th Ave. N.W.) is also worth the trip.

Fremont offers Outdoor Cinema each Saturday from June to Labor Day. Seating for these classic movies begins at 7 pm. If your trip to the city extends to the Summer Solstice, be sure to take in the Solstice Parade.

SEASONS AND TIMES
➤ Year-round: Daily. Most businesses and restaurants operate normal business hours.

COST
➤ Walking tour: Free. Fremont Outdoor Cinema: About $5 per person.

GETTING THERE
➤ By car, head east from Seattle Center on Mercer St. Turn north on Dexter Ave. and continue about 2 miles to the Fremont Bridge. Cross it into the heart of the Fremont district. About 10 minutes from Seattle Center.
➤ By public transit, take Metro bus 5, 26, 28, 31, 46, or 82 heading north from downtown Seattle. Call Metro Transit for route and schedule information (206) 553-3000.
➤ By bicycle, use the car directions.

NEARBY
➤ Lake Union, Green Lake, Ballard District, Burke-Gilman Bike Trail, Gas Works Park, University of Washington Campus.

COMMENT
➤ Bring a blanket and portable changing pad. Wear comfortable shoes. A backpack is preferable to a stroller in stores.

Fish and Ships
HIRAM
M. CHITTENDEN LOCKS

3015 N.W. 54th St., Seattle
(206) 783-7059
www.nws.usace.army.mil/opdiv/lwscl

At one of the area's best free attractions, engineering and nature share a double bill. The locks were created so watercraft could easily move between saltwater (Puget Sound) and freshwater (Lake Union) via the Ship Canal—built nearly 100 years ago. Vessels heading out to sea are "locked" between gates: the upper gate is on the city side with the lower gate leading to Puget Sound. Water is released from the locked area until it is level with Puget Sound. Then, the lower gate is opened and the vessels proceed out to sea. When returning, the process is reversed. Visitors can watch this engineering feat from above. Kids will enjoy observing the variety of boats and their occupants—from ocean kayaks to yachts to cruise boats.

Across the canal, a fish ladder with an underwater viewing window brings nature up close. After living in the sea for most of their lives, salmon return to their freshwater birthplace to spawn. The fish ladder assists them in their trip home. In the viewing area, interpretive displays describe the salmon's life cycle and help visitors identify the types of fish.

To learn more about the locks' operation and history, walk through the Visitor Center. Several of the exhibits are hands-on, including a working model of the locks that flashes red lights if you make a wrong move. A small bookstore (206-789-2622 ext. 320) sells books, postcards and other souvenirs. Take time to walk through the lovely Carl S. English Botanical Garden and enjoy a picnic on the lawn. In summer, free concerts are held on most Saturday and Sunday afternoons.

SEASONS AND TIMES
➤ Locks: Year-round, daily, 7 am–9 pm. Visitor Center: Summer (mid-May–mid-Sept), daily, 10 am–6 pm; Winter (mid-Sept–mid-May), Thu–Mon, 10 am–4 pm. Bookstore: Summer (May–Oct), daily, 11 am–5 pm; Winter (Oct–May), Thu–Mon, 11 am–4 pm.

COST
➤ Free.

GETTING THERE
➤ By car, take Denny Way westbound from Seattle Center and follow the road as it curves and turns into Elliott Ave. Follow Elliott northbound; it will become 15th St. N.W. Continue north on 15th across the Ballard Bridge to Market St. N.W. Turn west and continue to the Y in the road, following the signs to 54th St. N.W. Free parking on site. About 15 minutes from Seattle Center.

➤ By public transit. Call Metro Transit for route and schedule information (206) 553-3000.
➤ By bicycle, follow the car directions.

NEARBY
➤ Ballard and Fremont neighborhoods, Fishermen's Terminal, Discovery Park, Golden Gardens Park, Woodland Park Zoo, Nordic Heritage Museum.

COMMENT
➤ Plan a 1- to 2-hour visit.

See Winged Wonders at the MUSEUM OF FLIGHT

**9404 E. Marginal Way S., Seattle
(206) 764-5720
www.museumofflight.org**

With nicknames such as "Jet City" and "the city that Boeing built," it should not come as a surprise that Seattle is home to the west coast's largest air and space museum. For decades, airplane manufacturer, Boeing, was the area's largest employer. Although the Museum of Flight is not affiliated with Boeing, it's fitting that it's located at the site of the company's 1910 birthplace, the Red Barn.

The museum opened in 1983 with the Red Barn housing historical displays from the early days of flight. Since then, it has grown to include three floors of additional exhibits and activities. The Great Gallery showcases dozens of aircraft with some suspended from the ceiling of the six-story high building. It has a reconstructed full-size model of the Wright Brothers' 1902 glider, biplanes from World War II, the convertible "AeroCar II" (converts from a plane to a car in 10 minutes), the Blackbird spy plane and many other military, commercial and private aircraft.

Getting close to a variety of winged wonders is awe-inspiring for young visitors. Kids can climb into some of the planes in the Gallery. There are also some kid-size planes in the Hangar Room—a great spot to snap a photo of your young pilot. Every weekend, families can participate in hands-on workshops and learn about aerodynamics, while making paper airplanes, parachutes, rockets and other flying toys.

Hands-on fun awaits on the third floor too, where youngsters try their hand at being an air traffic controller as they listen to real controllers communicate at nearby Boeing Field. Outside, walk through the Air Force One jet, the plane that transported presidents Eisenhower, Kennedy and Nixon in the '50s and '60s. The Museum of Flight is also the Seattle base for the popular Blue Angels, the U.S. Navy's precision flying team, when they come to perform for the annual Seafair festival. Kids can meet the team at a free workshop at the museum in August.

SEASONS AND TIMES
→ Year-round: Daily, 10 am—5 pm (Thu until 9 pm). Closed Thanksgiving and Christmas.

COST
→ Adults $9.50, children (5 to 17) $5, under 5 free.

GETTING THERE

➤ By car, from Seattle Center, head east on Mercer St. to I-5 South. Take I-5 S. to Exit 158. Turn north at East Marginal Way S. The Museum is 1/2 mile north. Free parking on site. About 20 minutes from Seattle Center.

➤ By public transit, take Metro bus 174 from downtown Seattle or Sea-Tac Airport. Call Metro Transit for route and schedule information (206) 553-3000.

COMMENT

➤ Plan a 1- to 2-hour visit.

Hands-on Learning and Fun
PACIFIC SCIENCE CENTER

**200 – 2nd Ave. N., Seattle
(206) 443-2001
www.pacsci.org**

I f your kids think science is "boring" or "nerdy," one visit to the Pacific Science Center will change their minds. Originally built as the U.S. Science Pavilion for the 1962 Seattle World's Fair, the facility has been renovated and infused with interactive fun. The most stunning features of the original pavilion— five 110-foot arches that tower over terraced reflecting pools—still remain. Aside from the Space Needle, these arches are probably the most notable of the World's Fair's architectural legacies.

The exhibits have kept pace with the times. Tech Zone's computers, virtual reality games and robots interest both the tech-savvy and those just learning about the information age. For kids up to four feet tall, the Just for Tots area encourages science exploration via play equipment, books, puzzles and water play. In the Kids Works area, children of all ages can play with water, create music, dance with their own video image, freeze their shadow and view Seattle through a submarine periscope.

Other exhibits include life-size animatronic dinosaurs, a butterfly and insect village, body and health activities, a saltwater tide pool and outdoor water explorations. Planetarium shows are offered daily and temporary exhibits change seasonally. The center is also home to a Laser Theater and two IMAX™ theaters (page 123). Special festivals are held yearly, including the Model Railroad Show on Thanksgiving weekend, Science Wonderland during winter break and the Video Game Toy Test in August.

SEASONS AND TIMES
➤ Year-round: Mon—Fri, 10 am—5 pm; Sat—Sun, 10 am—6 pm. Closed Thanksgiving and Christmas.

COST
➤ Exhibits only: Adults $8, seniors (65 and up) and juniors (3 to 13) $5.50, under 3 free. IMAX™: $5.75 to $7.50. Laser Theatre: Fri-Sun, $7.50; Wed—Thu, $5. Combination admission prices available for exhibits and IMAX™ movies or Laser Shows.

GETTING THERE
➤ By car, from I-5 take the Mercer St. Exit and head west towards the Space Needle. Some free parking is available on nearby streets. During special events, parking fees at Center parking lots are based on the number of people in the vehicle (discounts for 2 or more). Expect to pay between $6 and $12 for all-day parking. Located at the south end of Seattle Center.
➤ By public transit, more than a dozen Metro bus routes service Seattle Center. Festival shuttles also run from several suburban park and ride lots during special events. Call Metro Transit for route and schedule information (206) 553-3000. Or ride the Monorail that travels between Seattle Center and downtown Seattle's Westlake Center.

NEARBY
➤ Seattle Center, downtown Seattle, Pike Place Market, Waterfront.

COMMENT
➤ Plan a 3- to 4-hour visit, to include an IMAX™ movie, Laser Show or planetarium program.

To Market, To Market
PIKE PLACE MARKET

Located between Pike and Bell just off 1st Ave., Seattle
(206) 682-7453 (Market Association)
www.pikeplacemarket.org

T he smells alone make you glad you came to Pike Place Market. The market's big draw is that it offers something for everyone and provides a wonderful cross-section of the city. First opened in 1907, Pike Place Market is the place for farmers to peddle their goods, locals to gather and tourists to find a blend of history, kitsch, fresh produce and street artists. Be warned if your kids are easily bored—there's not much to do at the market other than walk, eat and purchase goods, but that's the fun of it.

There are, however, a few "must do" activities for kids. Plunk a coin in the giant brass piggy bank, Rachel, located in the Main Arcade. Follow the pig hooves from the market entrance on Pike Street and you'll run right into the portly greeter. Next, turn around and watch the fish fly. The Pike Place Fish Shop is known around the world for its entertaining fishmongers. Their shouts of warning and delicate airborne fish ballet is a well-choreographed show. Don't miss the Heritage Center (1531 Western Ave.) to stock up on information about the market's long history.

In the North Arcade you'll find produce stands with local farmers offering samples of fresh berries, hunks of cheese and spoonfuls of honey. This is a great place to introduce a finicky eater to something new. While you stroll, be sure to see the hard-working street entertainers. Stop and watch their antics and let your kids drop a coin or two into their hats.

In the catacombs below the market there are a host of colorful kid-calling shops, chock-full of collectibles. Visit a magic shop; buy postcards, card-board stand-ups, star memorabilia and other gadgets from around the world. Shopping make you hungry? Why not buy some fresh produce and have a picnic at nearby Victor Steinbrueck Park.

SEASONS AND TIMES
➤ Year-round: Daily, Mon—Sat, 10 am—6 pm; Sun, 11 am—5 pm. Closed Christmas, New Year's, Easter and Thanksgiving. Individual business hours may vary.

COST
➤ Free. Bring plenty of cash for trinkets and enticing food. And a few extra dollars to tip street musicians and clowns.

GETTING THERE
➤ By car, from the south side of Seattle Center, head west on Denny Way. Turn south on 1st Ave. to Pike St. Pay parking garages nearby. About 3 minutes from Seattle Center.
➤ By public transit, take Metro bus 10 or 12 along 1st Ave. or other downtown buses on 2nd or 3rd Ave. and get off at Pike. Call Metro Transit for route and schedule information (206) 553-3000.

NEARBY
➤ Seattle Art Museum, Harbor Steps, Westlake Center, Waterfront, Benaroya Hall, Seattle Center.

COMMENT
➤ Backpacks are better than strollers. Bathrooms aren't the cleanest—bring a changing pad for use in Steinbrueck Park. Plan a 1- to 2-hour visit.

Out to the Ball Game at SAFECO FIELD

1200 – 1st Ave. S. at S. Royal Brougham Way, Seattle
(206) 346-4000
www.mariners.org/newpark

Seattle baseball fans were thrilled when Safeco Field opened as a world-class facility. Watching the Mariners play in open air on real grass is a vast improvement over the closed-in, artificial feeling of the former Kingdome. Baseball is meant to be played outdoors, yet thanks to a retractable roof, games don't get rained out. Still, you'll want to dress for the elements—even on a warm day, the wind can be brisk, making sweaters and blankets useful.

While seats in the bleachers can be had for as little as $5, there are more expensive temptations from tasty eats to souvenirs at the gift shop. To save money, bring a picnic from home (no cans or bottles). You can also enjoy the many free features the stadium offers, including the playground with its climbing equipment and tubes. Parents can watch their kids play from an adjacent area via TV monitors. If you decide to dine on Safeco Field fare, be prepared to make some decisions. This isn't just a hot dog and popcorn kind of place. Choices include fried chicken from Ezell's; an only-in-Seattle creation, the IvarDog (Ivar's fish in a hot dog bun); sushi and other Asian food; tacos; and barbecued meats from Bellevue-based Dixies.

SEASONS AND TIMES
➤ Season: Apr—Sept. Tours (1 hour): Apr—Oct, daily (when there are no games scheduled), 10:30 am, 12:30 pm and 2:30 pm. Nov—Mar, Tue—Sun, 12:30 pm and 2:30 pm.

COST
➤ Games: Tickets range from $5 to $32. Tours: Adults $7, seniors (65 and up) $5, children (3 to 12) $3, under 3 free.

GETTING THERE
➤ By car, from Seattle Center, head east on Mercer St. to I-5 South. Take I-5 S. to the Dearborn St. Exit and go west. Parking at the official Safeco Garage is $15; other private lots in the area charge between $12 and $20. About 10 minutes from Seattle Center.
➤ By public transit, there are more than 30 Metro bus routes that run within 3 blocks of the ballpark. Special shuttle buses operate from several outlying Park and Ride lots (including Northgate and Tukwila) on weekend game days; cost is $2.50 each way. Call Metro Transit for route and schedule information (206) 553-3000.

NEARBY
➤ Downtown Seattle, Pioneer Square, Waterfront, Chinatown/International District.

COMMENT
➤ With upwards of 30,000 fans at some games, it can feel like an eternity to inch through the traffic after a game. Rather than heading for the same freeway entrance as everyone else, try going south or north on 1st or 4th Ave. to access the freeway.

The Center of the Action
SEATTLE CENTER

🐝 🐝 🐝

**Just north of downtown, between 1st
and 5th avenues N., Denny and Mercer streets, Seattle
(206) 684-7200
www.seattlecenter.com**

C alled the "Century 21 Exposition" and held in 1962, the Seattle's World Fair focused on science, technology and the future, a theme expressed visually by the towering Space Needle (page 218) and the futuristic arches of today's Pacific Science Center (page 25). When the fair was over, Seattle Center was born—a ready-made civic center that included the Opera House, Monorail (page 212), Center House, International Fountain (page 84), Flag Pavilion and the Pacific Science Center. Today, the 74-acre site is one of the most popular visitor destinations in the U.S.

Its museums reflect this diversity. The Pacific Science Center offers hands-on learning for all ages while the Children's Museum (page 41) invites kids to explore life in a kid-size world. The Experience Music Project (page 17) attracts both rock 'n' roll fans and the stares of passers-by at its bizarre architectural design. For culture lovers, the center is home to Pacific Northwest Ballet (page 127), Seattle Opera, Seattle Children's Theatre (page 129) and more. There's also the Key Arena, site of major entertainment and sports events, Fun Forest Amusement Park (page 79) and Seattle Center House, a three-story building of restaurants and retail shops.

With all of these choices, visits can get expensive, but the center hosts many free events and attractions too. One popular spot for kids is the International Fountain, built for the fair and renovated in 1995. It shoots water 150 feet in the air from various nozzles. Also free are festivals (page 238), including Northwest Folklife, Bite of Seattle, Winterfest and Whirligig. Even Bumbershoot (page 233), the Labor Day arts and music festival, features dozens of performances and is free for ages 12 and under with a paying adult.

SEASONS AND TIMES
➤ Center grounds: Year-round, daily, 6:45 am—11 pm. Center House shops and restaurants: Sun—Tue, 11 am—6 pm; Wed—Sat, 11 am—8 pm.

COST
➤ Access to Seattle Center: Free except during Bumbershoot. Other attractions extra (see page listings above for details).

GETTING THERE
➤ By car, from I-5 take the Mercer St. Exit and head west towards the Space Needle. Some free parking is available on nearby streets. During special events, parking fees at Center parking lots are based on the number of people in the vehicle (discounts for 2 or more). Expect to pay from $6 to $12 for all-day parking. About 5 minutes from downtown Seattle.

➤ By public transit, more than a dozen Metro bus routes service Seattle Center. Festival shuttles also run from several suburban Park and Ride lots during special events. Call Metro Transit for route and schedule information (206) 553-3000. Or ride the Monorail that travels between Seattle Center and downtown Seattle's Westlake Center.

NEARBY
➤ Downtown Seattle, Waterfront, Pike Place Market.

COMMENT
➤ Plan to spend at least a full day here, or longer, if you have the time.

A *Shimmering Gateway*
THE WATERFRONT

Pier 50 to Myrtle Edwards Park, along Alaskan Way, Seattle
(206) 728-3000
www.portseattle.org/harbor/attraction

Seattle has several nicknames. Aside from "Coffee Capital of the World," "City by the Sound" is the most accurate, with the water from Puget Sound lapping at the city's western door. So, if you want to experience quintessential Seattle, a trip to the Waterfront is a must. Besides its significance in terms of the city's shipping history, the Waterfront is full of tourist attractions most kids adore. With the Olympic Mountain backdrop, the Waterfront is a treat for grown-ups too.

While browsing the tourist shops, be sure to visit Ye Olde Curiosity Shop (206-682-5894) located on Pier 54. Marked by its totem pole in the doorway, the shop has been captivating visitors with wall-to-wall thingamajigs since 1899. It is also home to not one, but two real mummies!

Boat tours abound along the Waterfront and are a great way to view the city's majestic skyline.

Washington State Ferries take off from Colman Dock and Terminal on Pier 50 (page 224). Argosy Cruises depart Piers 54 and 57 (page 228). The Tillicum Village Tour heads out from Piers 55 and 56 (page 113). Pier 54 Adventures (206-623-6364) offers speedboat tours of the harbor as well as a few slower options. For a longer journey, Victoria Clipper runs high-speed catamarans to Victoria, BC, and the San Juan Islands (206-448-5000).

Once on the Waterfront, don't miss the Seattle Aquarium (page 154) located on Pier 59. The aquarium offers terrific underwater views of beautiful Puget Sound. Across the street from the ferry dock, you'll notice a fleet of stairs heading up into the city. Harbor Steps' 16,000-square-foot staircase features eight waterfalls and leads to one of Seattle's best conversation pieces: the *Hammering Man* sculpture in front of Seattle Art Museum.

If little feet can't make it up those stairs, make a beeline for Pier 66 and one of Seattle's newest hands-on museums. Odyssey: The Maritime Discovery Center is designed to teach visitors young and old about Seattle's long sea commerce history. Round out your day with a ride on the carousel located inside Pier 57.

SEASONS AND TIMES
→ Year-round: Daily. Boat tour and ferry times vary seasonally.

COST
→ Free. See pages listed above for specific cost information.

GETTING THERE

➻ From the east side of Seattle Center, take Broad St. west towards Puger Sound. Turn south on Alaskan Way and continue to parking lots between Piers 50-66. About 5 minutes from Seattle Center.

➻By public transit, take Metro Buses 10, 12 or 7 to Pike Place Market. Call Metro Transit for route and schedule information (206) 553-3000. Take the Market elevator or the steps down to waterfront. The Waterfront Streetcar (Route 99) runs along the Waterfront to Pioneer Square and the International District.

NEARBY

➻ Seattle Center, Westlake Center, Pioneer Square, Pike Place Market, Seattle Art Museum.

COMMENT

➻ Strollers or backpacks are a must with small kids. The Waterfront can be packed especially in summer, so decide on a "lost-and-found" meeting place (the Aquarium is a good choice). Plan a 2- to 3-hour visit, not counting boat trips.

CHAPTER 2

MUSEUMS

Introduction

I f you think museums are stuffy, boring and not very "kid-friendly," it's time to reconsider. Nowadays they are stocked with hands-on exhibits, unique and quirky displays and many offer classes and events geared for families. In Seattle, most museums are downright fun to explore. One of Seattle's best is the Children's Museum at Seattle Center, a must-visit for the under-12 crowd. There's plenty of fun for grown-ups too.

At the Museum of History & Industry, learn about Seattle's cultural and social history, including the great fire of 1889. Local law enforcement since the mid-1800s is chronicled at the Seattle Metropolitan Police Museum. The Wing Luke Asian Museum and Nordic Heritage Museum highlight the history, accomplishments and culture of some of the earlier settlers.

If dinosaurs are more your thing, visit the Burke Museum of Natural History and Culture. Budding artists will find inspiration and instruction at the Seattle Art Museum and Seattle Asian Art Museum. Doll lovers won't want to miss the Rosalie Whyel Museum of Doll Art. If that's not enough, check out the list of "other museums," which offers more destinations for exploring culture, industry, art and the military.

NOTE
Museums covered in chapters one, four and nine of this guide also welcome children.

Dinosaur Delights
BURKE MUSEUM
OF NATURAL HISTORY
AND CULTURE

Corner of 17th Ave. N.E. and N.E. 45th St., Seattle
(206) 543-5590
www.washington.edu/burkemuseum

C ruising along Highway 99 not long ago, you would have encountered a billboard featuring a dinosaur skeleton with the caption "What Barney Looks Like Inside." Adults can talk about prehistoric Earth until they are blue in the face and not make a five year old understand. But finding out what one of television's most popular characters looks like inside with one picture, now that's perfect bait!

You get to see a lot more than a stuffed dino's innards at the Burke. The museum offers families a wonderful introduction to Washington's archeological and cultural history. The first floor exhibits feature dinosaurs, a huge marine reptile called an elasmosaur and a batch of life-size dinosaur eggs. Many of the displays in the first floor Life and Times of Washington State exhibit are interactive. You can step right into the impression of a dinosaur foot or walk through a volcano to better understand what's brewing in Mount Rainier.

The Pacific Voices exhibit does not offer the same hands-on experience. But many young people are still captivated by the masks, boats and garb of Pacific Northwest Native American tribes. This is the real stuff—an impressive collection of artifacts, art and information. The museum has special events, traveling exhibits, educational classes and workshops for kids and adults, and family fun days throughout the year. Be sure to check out the annual Dinosaur Day event. It is a favorite with kids offering them hands-on activities, demonstrations and a chance to talk to experts about the prehistoric creatures that once roamed Earth.

SEASONS AND TIMES
➤ Year-round: Daily, 10 am–5 pm (Thu until 8 pm).

COST
➤ Suggested donation: Adults $5.50, seniors $4., students and children $2.50. Annual family memberships available. Complimentary admission for museum members, children under 6 and UW students and faculty.

GETTING THERE
➤ By car, from Seattle Center, head east on Mercer St. to I-5 North. Take I-5 N. to the N.E. 45th St. Exit and follow N.E. 45th heading east to 17th Ave. N.E. Turn into the northeast University of Washington entrance. The museum is visible immediately upon entering the campus. Look for pay parking in the lot adjacent to the museum (free on Sundays). About 10 minutes from Seattle Center.
➤ By public transit, take Metro bus 71, 72, or 73 from the Seattle bus tunnel (downtown at Westlake Center). Call Metro Transit for route and schedule information (206) 553-3000.

NEARBY
➤ University of Washington, Green Lake, Gas Works Park, Burke-Gilman Trail, Museum of History & Industry, Arboretum.

COMMENT
➤ Plan a 2-hour visit.

Play All Day
CHILDREN'S MUSEUM

**Center House (lower level at Seattle Center),
305 Harrison St., Seattle
(206) 441-1768
www.thechildrensmuseum.org**

Around the world in two hours? The Children's Museum at Seattle Center makes the educational and entertaining trip possible for imaginative youngsters. This is hands-on learning at its best, with costumes, games, authentic instruments, real mechanics and loads of information at every turn.

The fun starts in the hallway outside the entrance. Kids are invited to change the patterned hallway lighting with the push of a button. Once inside, little ones make a beeline to the Mountain Forest exhibit where they hunt for animal tracks under rocks, or clamber up the peak and "camp out" in the tent.

Back at sea level, the museum's Global Village is an exploration of world cultures. Cubby after cubby feature pint-size stores, homes, streets and other representations of life—from the Metro bus and European grocery store, to a Japanese-style home and Mexican restaurant. Do not overlook the theater and stage where kids can dress up, set the lighting and put on a show.

On the other side of the museum stands Cog City, a towering, noisy, hands-on physics lesson comprised of levers, pulleys, balls and cogs. The artist studio offers school-age children the chance to create works of art with real artists in residence. A computerized technology lab and music recording studio are a lure for older kids.

The museum offers workshops, storytelling circles and special events year-round. Call for upcoming events. Like most indoor attractions, the museum is packed on rainy days. Try visiting on a weekday when the crowds are less overwhelming.

SEASONS AND TIMES
➤ Year-round: Mon—Fri, 10 am—5 pm; Sat—Sun, 10 am—6 pm.

COST
➤ $5 per person. Memberships available.

GETTING THERE
➤ By car, from I-5 take the Mercer St. Exit and head west to Seattle Center. The 1st N. Garage and Lot 4 are located on the west side of Seattle Center. During special events, parking fees at Center lots are based on the number of people in the vehicle (discounts for 2 or more). Expect to pay from $6 to $12 for all-day parking.
➤ By public transit, ride the Monorail that travels between Seattle Center and downtown Seattle's Westlake Center. More than a dozen Metro bus routes service Seattle Center. Call Metro Transit for route and schedule information (206) 553-3000.

NEARBY
➤ Seattle Center and Space Needle, The Opera House, downtown Seattle, Waterfront, Queen Anne Hill, Experience Music Project.

COMMENT
➤ Plan at least a 2-hour visit.

SIMILAR ATTRACTIONS
➤ **Children's Museum of Snohomish County** · 3013 Colby Ave., Everett (425) 258-1006 www.childs-museum.org
➤ **Children's Museum of Tacoma** · 936 Broadway, Tacoma (253) 627-6031.

Discover Seattle's Past
MUSEUM OF HISTORY & INDUSTRY

2700 – 24th Ave. E., Seattle
(206) 324-1126
www.mohai.org

What was Seattle like when it was first settled in the 1800s? Find out at the Museum of History & Industry. Take a walk through the Seattle in the 1880s exhibit and see a general store, millinery, blacksmith, bank, saloon, barber shop and other businesses. Each is complete with tools and products from that era. In the Seattle Roots exhibit, pick up a nametag and pretend to be a historic character as you look at displays that describe Seattle from the 1850s to the present.

In the interactive Salmon Stakes exhibit, visitors learn firsthand about the importance of salmon in our region. Kids can climb into a fishing boat, haul in salmon, operate a canning mechanism and peek into a bunkhouse. They can also visit the Great Seattle Fire exhibit and learn how firefighters battled the blazing city in 1889.

From Thanksgiving to New Year's, the museum presents Home for the Holidays, a nostalgic display of antique toys and decorations. The Saturday after Thanksgiving is Holiday History Market Day and admission is free. The museum also offers a variety of weekend programs for families, including story-telling on Sundays and craft workshops held the first Saturday of each month.

If you have time left over, explore nearby Foster Island. A pathway to the east of the museum's lower parking lot leads to a network of planks and footbridges built over a marshy island.

SEASONS AND TIMES
➤ Year-round: Daily, 10 am—5 pm. Closed Thanksgiving, Christmas, New Year's.

COST
➤ General $5.50, seniors (over 55) and children (6 to 12) $3, tots (2 to 5) $1, under 2 free.

GETTING THERE
➤ By car, from Seattle Center, head east on Mercer St. to I-5 North. Take I-5 N. to Exit 168B to SR-520. Follow SR-520 east and exit at Montlake Blvd. Go 1 block to 24th Ave. E. and turn north to the museum. From westbound SR-520, take the Lake Washington Blvd. Exit and proceed west. Turn north on 24th Ave. E. Free parking on site. About 10 minutes from Seattle Center.
➤ By public transit, more than 26 buses stop near the museum at Montlake Station. Call Metro Transit for route and schedule information (206) 553-3000.

NEARBY
➤ University of Washington, Arboretum, Burke Museum of Natural History and Culture, University Village Shopping Center.

COMMENT
➤ Plan a 1- to 2-hour visit.

Seattle's Norse Connection
NORDIC HERITAGE MUSEUM

**3014 N.W. 67th St., Seattle
(206) 789-5707
www.nordicmuseum.com**

Driving down the streets in Seattle, you're apt to run into bumper stickers sporting the message "Uff Da!" (which means "Uh Oh!"). Chances are the driver is a proud member of Seattle's large Nordic community. In the early 1900s, Swedes, Finns, Norwegians and Icelanders immigrated to the city to take advantage of the fishing industry. As they settled in what is now called the Ballard neighborhood, the immigrants became a defining element of the city's character. The laid-back, open-arm Nordic style remains one of the city's dominant traits today.

There is no better place than Ballard to erect the only museum in the U.S. that is devoted to Nordic history. The Nordic Heritage Museum offers visitors a colorful, interactive look at Nordic immigration and Ballard's important role in Seattle's past.

The museum's centerpiece is a life-size exhibit covering three floors and depicting the Scandinavians' journey to America. Visitors can walk through the hull of a great ship and along turn-of-the-century city streets. Check out the shops, stores, canneries, fishing boats and implements of the early immigrants and read about their hardships and triumphs. Try to plan your visit around the museum's many annual children's events, such as a birthday salute to Hans Christian Andersen, Tivoli-Viking Days, an Easter celebration, Yulefest, a visit by Halloween trolls or Children's Christmas in Scandinavia.

The museum offers classes and other activities on all things Nordic throughout the year. Call ahead for a schedule and times. If it is a nice day, pack a lunch and have a picnic at the museum park, located on the northwest corner, just outside the main entrance.

SEASONS AND TIMES
➛ Year-round: Tue—Sat, 10 am—4 pm; Sun, noon—4 pm.

COST
➛ Adults $4, seniors and students $3, children (5 to 17) $2, under 5 free.

GETTING THERE
➛ By car, from Seattle Center, head east on Mercer St. to I-5 North. Take the I-5 N. to N. 45th St. Exit and head west on N. 45th. It will eventually wind downhill and turn into Market St. Follow Market to 32nd Ave. N.W. and turn north onto 32nd. Look for signs to the museum around N.W. 65th St. Free parking on site. About 15 minutes from Seattle Center.
➛ By public transit, take Metro bus 17 from the Seattle bus tunnel (downtown at Westlake Center). Call Metro Transit for route and schedule information (206) 553-3000.

NEARBY
➛ Ballard, Hiram M. Chittenden Locks, Shilshole Bay, Golden Gardens Park.

COMMENT
➛ Plan a 1-hour visit. Longer if you want to play in the park.

Hello, Dolly
ROSALIE WHYEL
MUSEUM OF DOLL ART

1116 - 108th Ave. N. E., Bellevue
(425) 455-1116
www.dollart.com

Y ou find dolls in lots of museums. After all, kids have been playing with them for centuries. But it is rare to see so many dolls, from such a range of eras, all in one place.

The Rosalie Whyel Museum is a 13,000-square-foot, $3.5-million Victorian mansion and home to 3,000 dolls on permanent display. Some of the most stunning date back to the 1600s. The museum's collection includes a huge array of toys, as well as miniatures, dollhouses, bears and other childhood memorabilia. Also on display are two ancient Egyptian tomb dolls that were buried with dead kings.

Visitors have the opportunity to learn about the long history of doll making and leave with a better understanding and appreciation of the artistry behind the work. The museum offers numerous doll-making workshops throughout the year. They also sponsor special educational events, a newsletter and a website listing upcoming doll shows across the country.

On the website, museum staff cite the best reason to put the doll museum on your list: "For adults, dolls evoke a great sense of nostalgia. For children, they show the child's world is important."

SEASONS AND TIMES
➤ Year-round: Mon—Sat, 10 am—5 pm; Sun, 1 pm—5 pm.

COST
➤ Adults $7, seniors $6, children (5 to 17) $5, under 5 free. Discounts for groups and AAA members.

GETTING THERE
➤ By car, from Seattle Center, head east on Mercer St. to I-5 North. Take the I-5 N. to the SR-520 Exit and proceed east to I-405 S. Go south on I-405 to the N.E. 8th St .Westbound Exit, then go west to 108th Ave. N.E. and turn north. The museum is on the corner of N.E. 12th and 108th N.E. Free parking on site. About 20 minutes from Seattle Center.
➤ By public transit, take Sound Transit 550 Express from the Seattle bus tunnel (downtown at Westlake Center). Call Metro Transit for route and schedule information (206) 553-3000.

NEARBY
➤ Bellevue Art Museum, Bellevue Downtown Park, Meydenbauer Parks, Bellevue Square.

COMMENT
➤ Plan a 1- to 2-hour visit.

Making Art at the
SEATTLE ART MUSEUM

100 University St., Seattle
(206) 654-3100
www.seattleartmuseum.org

The Seattle Art Museum (SAM) is easy to find—thanks to the massive 48-foot *Hammering Man* statue that stands guard outside. The museum spans five floors and is jam-packed with art from around the world. It has more than 23,000 objects, from ancient Egyptian reliefs to modern day photography and videos. The main collections include examples of African and Northwest Coast Native American art, modern works, European painting, sculpture and decorative arts.

SAM has a strong commitment to education of all kinds. Families can learn in the Please Touch room on the third floor. In the Special Exhibition Galleries, Family Fun Packs are available—containing games and activities geared to preschool children. Family Days, featuring entertainment and workshops relating to the museum's special exhibits, and art studio classes and tours are held throughout the year.

To enhance your family's visit, check out SAM's website. It has interactive games and stories, lesson plans for teachers and on-line tours of some collections. Don't miss My Art Gallery, where kids can make their own on-line exhibition using virtual art from the museum.

SEASONS AND TIMES
➤ Year-round: Tue—Sun, 10 am—5 pm (Thu until 9 pm). Open holiday Mondays. Closed Thanksgiving, Christmas, New Year's.

COST
➤ Adults $7, seniors (over 61) and students $5, children under 12 free (when accompanied by an adult). First Thursday of every month is free. First Friday of every month free for seniors. Take your ticket stub to the Seattle Asian Art Museum (page 51) within 1 week of your visit and receive free admission.

GETTING THERE
➤ By car, from Seattle Center, head west on Broad St. to 1st Ave., turn south and proceed to museum on the northeast corner of 1st and University St. Pay and metered parking nearby. About 5 minutes from Seattle Center.
➤ By public transit, take Metro bus 10 or 12 along 1st Ave. or other downtown buses that run on 2nd or 3rd Ave. Get off at University. Call Metro Transit for route and schedule information (206) 553-3000.

NEARBY
➤ Pike Place Market, Pioneer Square, Waterfront, Seattle Aquarium, Westlake Center and downtown shopping.

COMMENT
➤ Plan a 1- to 2-hour visit.

Exploring Asia at the
SEATTLE ASIAN
ART MUSEUM

1400 E. Prospect St., Seattle
(206) 654-3100
www.seattleartmuseum.org

This impressive art deco building was built in 1933 to house a Seattle family's Asian art collection and was once home to the Seattle Art Museum. The museum was renovated in 1991 (after the Seattle Art Museum moved to its downtown locale) and now focuses solely on Asian art.

Start your visit by examining the museum's collection of Japanese art, featuring examples of calligraphy, ink painting, Buddhist and folk art, ceramics and folk textiles. Stop in at the Chinese collection with its tomb figures, textiles, jade carvings, metalwork, Buddhist sculpture and more than 350 Chinese puppets. The museum has fine examples of Korean and South and Southeast Asian art (including folding screens), Thai ceramics, Hindu sculptures and more.

At the interactive exhibit, Explore Korea: A Visit to Grandfather's House, visitors journey through a traditional Korean house. Each room has objects to discover and activities, such as board games, calligraphy, clothes to try on and kitchen fun. In the art workshop, kids ages five to ten can make crafts to take home. The museum offers special events too, including concerts and family programs. The tearoom is a great place to introduce children to some of Asia's culinary treats.

After the visit, if it's a nice day, plan to climb the 75 steps up Volunteer Park's water tower for an excellent view of the city. To warm up in cooler weather, walk to the nearby Victorian botanical conservatory (206-684-7438). Admission is free and the warmth, scents and colorful plants are quite pleasant. The park also has a play area, wading pool and concert bandstand.

SEASONS AND TIMES
➤ Year-round: Tue—Sun, 10 am—5 pm (Thu until 9 pm). Open holiday Mondays. Closed Thanksgiving, Christmas and New Year's.

COST
➤ Adults $3, children (under 12) free when accompanied by an adult. First Thursday and Saturday of every month free. First Friday of every month free for seniors. Take your ticket stub to the Seattle Art Museum (page 49) within 1 week of your visit and receive free admission.

GETTING THERE
➤ By car, take Denny Way east from Seattle Center to Olive Way. Continue east to 15th Ave. E. and turn north. At E. Prospect St., turn west at the park entrance and follow the signs to the museum. From I-5 northbound, take the Olive Way Exit and follow the Olive Way instructions above. From I-5 southbound, take the Roanoke St. Exit and go east to 10th Ave. E. Turn south and go to Boston Ave. E., turn east and continue to the park entrance. Free parking on site. About 10 minutes from Seattle Center.
➤ By public transit, take Metro bus 10 into Volunteer Park. Call Metro Transit for schedule information (206) 553-3000.

NEARBY
➤ Volunteer Park, Capitol Hill neighborhood, Seattle Center, downtown Seattle, Museum of History & Industry, Arboretum.

COMMENT
➤ Plan a 1- to 2-hour visit, including time for the park.

"Wanted" at the
SEATTLE METROPOLITAN POLICE MUSEUM

317 – 3rd Ave. S., Seattle
(206) 748-9991
http://members.aol.com/smpmuseum

Visitors learn all about the history of Seattle and King County's law enforcement at this museum. Exhibits dating to the 1860s include antique firearms, uniforms, badges, photographs, newspaper clippings, old mug books, "wanted" posters and more.

See displays of handcuffs, leg irons and other paraphernalia that were once used to restrain prisoners. You'll learn about some of the police department's more notorious activities, including corruption, riots and lynching. In the hands-on area, kids can try on police uniforms and equipment—such as gun belts, bulletproof vests, hats and helmets—and see how official they look in the mirror. There is also a police light to turn on, a communications center where kids can pretend to be a 911 dispatcher and a 1950s-style jail cell that visitors can step inside. Groups can call ahead to arrange a special tour with Officer Ritter, the Seattle police officer who started the museum several years ago. These tours can include visits with officers from the K-9, Crime Prevention or SWAT teams.

SEASONS AND TIMES
➤ Year-round: Tue—Sat, 11 am—4 pm.

COST
➤ Adults $3, children (under 13) $1.50.

GETTING THERE
➤ By car, from Seattle Center, head east on Mercer St. to I-5 South. Take I-5 S. to the James St. Exit and go west. Turn south on 5th Ave., then west at S. Jackson St. and proceed to 3rd Ave. S. There is metered street parking and nearby pay lots. About 10 minutes from Seattle Center.
➤ By public transit, take southbound Metro bus 7, 14 or 36 along 3rd and get off at S. Jackson. Call Metro Transit for route and schedule information (206) 553-3000.

NEARBY
➤ Pioneer Square, International District, Waterfront, Safeco Field, Wing Luke Asian Museum, Klondike Gold Rush Historical Park.

COMMENT
➤ Plan a 1-hour visit.

Going International
WING LUKE ASIAN MUSEUM

407 – 7th Ave. S., Seattle
(206) 623-5124
www.wingluke.org

This small but informative museum in the International District showcases the history of Asians and Pacific Islanders in the Seattle area. It opened in 1967 and was named after Wing Luke—the first Asian American to hold elected office in the Pacific Northwest when he joined the Seattle City Council in 1962. Over the years, the local community has helped develop the museum.

The main exhibit, One Song, Many Voices, depicts 200 years of immigration and settlement. It integrates the stories of ten Asian Pacific American groups—Cambodians, Chinese, Filipinos, Japanese, Koreans, Laotians, Pacific Islanders, South Asians, Southeast Asian hill tribes and Vietnamese. You will see displays of costumes and tools, as well as musical instruments, photographs and other unique items. An exhibit about the internment of Japanese-Americans during World War II is especially thought-provoking, as it provides an opportunity to educate children about racial injustice.

The International District's own unique multi-cultural history is represented by artifacts, signs and photos. Hanging from the museum's rafters are items of special appeal to children: hand painted animal kites, a 35-foot Chinese dragon kite and a 50-foot dragon boat. The museum offers a number of events, workshops, tours, concerts and family programs.

SEASONS AND TIMES
→ Year-round: Tue—Fri, 11 am—4:30 pm; Sat—Sun, noon—4 pm.

COST
→ Adults $4, seniors and students $3, children (5 to 12) $2, under 5 free. Free admission on first Thursday of each month.

GETTING THERE
→ By car, from Seattle Center, head east on Mercer St. to I-5 South. Take I-5 S. to the Dearborn St. Exit and drive west toward Safeco Field,

turn north on 7th Ave. and drive for 3 blocks. Park at the pay lot on Jackson St. between 8th and 9th Ave. or on the street. About 10 minutes from Seattle Center.

➤ By public transit, board any southbound bus at the Seattle bus tunnel (downtown at Westlake Center). Get off at the International District station. Walk east along Jackson, then turn south on 7th. Alternatively, board southbound bus 7, 14 or 36 along 3rd Ave. and get off at Maynard St. and Jackson. Walk east along Jackson to 7th and turn south. Call Metro Transit for route and schedule information (206) 553-3000.

NEARBY
➤ Chinatown/International District, Safeco Field, Pioneer Square, Seattle Metropolitan Police Museum.

COMMENT
➤ Plan a 45-minute visit.

Other Museums

African American Museum
925 Court C, Tacoma
(253) 274-1278
www.aamuseumtacoma.org

Thousands of artifacts and photos depict the lives of African-Americans in the Pacific Northwest. Permanent exhibits highlight African-American pioneers, state mayors and military service.

Coast Guard Museum Northwest
1519 Alaskan Way S., Seattle
(206) 217-6993

The museum showcases Coast Guard uniforms and equipment, nautical items and models of ships. There is a working lighthouse mechanism. When Coast Guard vessels are in port, tours are often available. Free.

Fort Lewis Military Museum
Bldg. 4320, Main St., Fort Lewis
(253) 967-7206

Housed in a historic structure built in the World War I era, the museum displays military vehicles, army uniforms, equipment and artifacts dating from 1804 to the present. Free.

Frye Art Museum
704 Terry Ave., Seattle
(206) 622-9250
www.fryeart.org

The museum has a collection of 19th and 20th century paintings and temporary exhibits by contemporary painters. Free. Classes and workshops for children and families are provided for an additional cost.

Henry Art Gallery
15th Ave. N.E. and N.E. 41st St., Seattle
(206) 543-2280
www.henryart.org

The University of Washington's art museum features modern and contemporary art from around the world. Students with ID and children under 1 free. Free for everyone on Thursdays between 5 and 8 pm.

McChord Air Force Base Museum
McChord Air Force Base (Exit 125 off I-5), Tacoma
(253) 984-2485

Learn about the Air Force and see planes and equipment at this military museum. Free.

Suquamish Museum
15838 Sandy Hook Rd., Suquamish
(360) 598-3311 ext. 422
www.telebyte.com/suquamish/museum

Highly acclaimed Native American historical museum on the Kitsap Peninsula.

Tacoma Art Museum
1123 Pacific Ave. Tacoma
(253) 272-4258
www.tacomaartmuseum.org

The museum's ArtWORKS interactive art-making studio is fun for families. Special programs and classes for children are offered. The museum features works by Northwest artists—including glass artists—and traveling exhibits.

Vintage Telephone Equipment Museum
7000 E. Marginal Way S. (in US West building), Seattle
(206) 767-3012
www.scn.org/tech/telmuseum/index.html

The museum highlights the history of telephones with equipment dating back to 1876. Kids can crank phones, learn how switches work, play "stump the computer" and pretend they are telephone operators. Open Tuesdays 9 am to 2 pm and by appointment.

CHAPTER 3

IN YOUR NEIGHBORHOOD

Introduction

In family-friendly Seattle, you don't need to travel far to find attractions and activities that interest kids. Some of the best places are in your own neighborhood and are free or low-cost.

This chapter includes a variety of ideas for outings—farmer's markets, painting studios, craft shops, bowling alleys and other everyday places where a little imagination can turn an ordinary trip into a fun-filled adventure. Did you know that community centers in Seattle have family skate nights? Have you watched movies at Issaquah's public swimming pool's "Dive In"? This chapter also tells you about one of the best sources for free entertainment—your local library, which offers storytelling, craft and drama programs.

The following listings are meant to introduce you to the possibilities for family fun in your neck of the woods and invite you to explore other neighborhoods. In this chapter, you'll find a few specific suggestions to get you started and places where you can find more information. For a quick overview of local services and attractions for families by region, visit www.localmom.com/Seattle.

Rainy Day
BOWLING ALLEYS

(206) 923-3138 (Greater Seattle Bowling Association)
(253) 941-3535 (Youth Bowling Association)
(206) 878-4669 (Women's Bowling Association)

Of course it rains in Seattle; it also snows, hails and can be foggy some days. Keeping a cache of nasty-weather activities the entire family can enjoy is not only smart, but also necessary. Bowling is an ideal outing for children of all ages and their parents. Even toddlers will have fun rolling the ball—even if they play by their own rules. More than just fun, it's inexpensive (around $1 to $3 a game per person, plus shoe rental). There are only a handful of bowling alleys within Seattle city limits, but surrounding communities such as Kent, Lynnwood, Burien and Edmonds help fatten the list. Most alleys offer instruction, leagues for players of all ages and often host special and seasonal events—Halloween Bowling, Mom's Night Out and Dad and Me, to name a few.

If you have older children, a regular lane and a lightweight ball are all you need for a roaring good time. If your family includes smaller kids, consider a game of bumper bowling. Many Seattle-area alleys install gutter pads that enable even the youngest bowler to get the ball to the pins. Call before you head out to find out what family activities are on the menu.

Looking for the best? Sunset Bowl offers birthday parties for kids and some great holiday events—check out the Thanksgiving open bowl in

November or the Christmas Eve Bowling Party.
Their youth bowling league promises no one "sits on
the bench!"

AMF IMPERIAL LANES
2101 – 22nd Ave. S., Seattle (206) 325-2525
Birthday parties, Extreme Bowling (glow-in-the-dark
bowling), youth league.

LEILANI LANES
10201 Greenwood Ave. N., Seattle (206) 783-8010
www.leilanilanes.com
Birthday parties, spare time parties for adolescents,
game room, youth league.

SKYWAY PARK BOWL
11819 Renton Ave. S., Seattle (206) 772-1220
www.skywaypark.com
Birthday parties, youth leagues, automated bumpers,
18-hole indoor mini-golf course.

SUNSET BOWL
1420 N.W. Market St., Seattle (206) 782-7310
Birthday parties, holiday theme days, youth league.

WEST SEATTLE BOWL
4505 – 39th Ave. S.W., Seattle (206) 932-3731
Birthday parties, GlowZone rock-n-roll bowl on
Saturday nights, youth league, holiday theme parties.

Local Treasure Chests
CHILDREN'S LIBRARIES

Visit any public library in the greater Seattle area and you'll find a section devoted to children. These days they contain more than books and cozy corners. Your kids will have access to games, toys, music, interactive computers and Internet facilities. Libraries have story times for toddlers, preschoolers and families, Spanish/English bilingual story times, book clubs and many special events and activities for children throughout the year. Summer programs feature free shows by noted children's entertainers and free workshops on crafts, drama, science and more. The theme changes each summer, but programs always include prizes for kids who reach their reading goals.

Seattle Public Library (206-386-4636; www.spl.org) includes the downtown Central Library and 26 branches. Kids can get their own library cards and borrow books, videos, CDs and magazines for up to three weeks. No overdue fines are charged on children's material checked out by kids or adults. The King County Library System (1-800-462-9600; www.kcls.org) spans the region with 41 libraries. Most items (except magazines and videos) can be checked out for four weeks and renewed for two more. Fines for most late items are ten cents per day. All of the libraries have on-line catalogs for searching and reserving books and other items. These items are then sent to the nearest library for you to pick up. Their websites also offer extensive resources for kids and parents, including homework help, on-line databases and an e-mail reference service where library members can fill out an "Ask a Librarian" form.

Recreation Abounds at
COMMUNITY CENTERS

The fun never stops at Seattle's 24 community centers. Parents can socialize while toddlers amuse themselves at indoor play centers. These centers are open one or more days per week during the winter season. Families can partake in a wide variety of recreational activities, including Family Skate Night, Movie Night, Game Night, Contra Dancing and more. The centers also offer classes for kids and adults, including cooking, arts and crafts, sports, dance and music, as well as day camps, pre-school programs and teen get-togethers.

To see a complete list of the centers, look in the blue pages of the phone book under "Seattle City of," then "Parks & Recreation Department," then "Community Centers." Or look on-line at www.ci.seattle. wa.us/parks/Centers/index.htm. Community recreation centers are also found in nearby cities including Shoreline, Bellevue, Kirkland, Redmond, Kent and Mountlake Terrace. Check the blue pages of the phone book under "Parks and Recreation" for information.

Party Central
COSTUMES, SUPPLIES
AND INVITES

Picture aisle upon aisle of wigs, boas, glitter, gowns, hero garb, popular character faces (including several past presidents) and full-body costumes. Whether you are looking to add to your family's dress-up box or throw the perfect party, several Seattle merchants stand ready to help you turn your dream persona or party into a reality.

As in every business, some stores are better than others. Two costume centers stand out in the crowd for their incredibly diverse inventory and helpful staff. If you want to find everything you need for your party at one stop, make it Display & Costume in North Seattle or Champion Party Supply near Seattle Center. These two stores combined could outfit every kid in the city. Call ahead to ask about specific costumes or supplies—employees are eager to help. If you can't find what you need at these two locations, go on-line to www.seattle.citysearch.com and read about the 13 Places to Find Killer Costumes. Or look in the yellow pages for dozens of other possibilities under "Party Supplies and Costumes."

ARCHIE MCPHEE AND CO.
2428 N.W. Market St., Seattle
(206) 297-0240

BROCKLIND'S COSTUME COMPANY
500 E. Pike St., Seattle
(206) 325-8700

CHAMPION PARTY SUPPLY
124 Denny Way, Seattle
(206) 284-1980

DISPLAY & COSTUME
11201 Roosevelt Way N.E., Seattle
(206) 362-4810

Beads, Boxes and Things
CRAFTY PLACES

Washington State Arts Commission
(206) 753-3860

There are numerous outlets available to help set your family's creative juices flowing in Seattle. The city boasts a number of shops specializing in beads, baubles, art and craft supplies, and how-to manuals for just about every art form. If cleaning up after your family's crafty foray deters you, however, read on for other options.

The Children's Museum at Seattle Center (page 41) gets children and families excited and engaged in art making through its outstanding artist-in-residence program. The museum's hands-on art workshops teach children of all ages the basics while helping them understand the genius of art greats like Chagall.

The Creation Station in Lynnwood is not only a young artisan's haven, it is an environmentalist's dream. The shop is filled with basic household and office items that really set a child's imagination on fire—ribbons, toilet paper tubes, straws, buttons and bows, paper clips and PVC pipe to name a few. All materials are recycled and were saved from a landfill by Creation Station proprietors. Along with the mounds of recyclables, Creation Station staff have great ideas to kick start your family's artistic or practical craft masterpiece. At about $5 per project per child, Creation Station is hours of fun and light on the wallet.

Offering award-winning art classes since 1982, Neo Art boasts a wide curriculum taught by artist-teachers from diverse backgrounds and art specialties. All programs use non-toxic materials and are designed to enhance a child's or adult's creative development and environmental awareness. The school offers seasonal camps, parent-child classes and more. The Children's Museum, Creation Station and Neo Art are great places for birthday parties too. For information on local or county art commissions, go to the blue pages in your telephone directory under City or County headings.

CREATION STATION
19511 – 64th Ave. W., Lynnwood
(425) 775-7959

CHILDREN'S MUSEUM
Center House, Seattle Center
(206) 441-1768

NEO ART SCHOOL
4649 Sunnyside Ave. N.
(206) 632-2530

ON-LINE BEAD STORE DIRECTORY
www.members.home.net/sdsantan/washington.html

Fresh Produce
FARMER'S MARKETS

Low on groceries? Why not make your next shop for family staples an entertaining and educational adventure. Seattle's farmer's markets offer the chance to do that—purchase fruits, vegetables and other products direct from the growers and talk to them about their work. Your family will learn to appreciate fresh food for its beauty, superior taste and healthy qualities. While the cost of some products is higher when purchased directly from the farmer, a trip to a market generally means food savings. And where prices are a wash, the freshness and quality of the produce, as well as the open-air market atmosphere, make supermarket shopping pale in comparison.

Seattle-area markets differ widely in size and scope. A trip to Pike Place Market downtown can be a daylong excursion as you explore candy shops, vegetable stands, meat markets and a slew of trinket shops. Artisans and entertainers are set up on every street corner and draw large crowds in the summer.

Smaller markets, such as the Columbia City Farmer's Market, University District Farmer's Market, Fremont Sunday Flea Market and West Seattle Market offer the same fresh produce, friendly merchants, talented entertainers and artisans, neighborly gossip and a chance to get out and explore some of the city's oldest communities. No matter which market your family frequents, you can count on one thing— each trip is an invitation to step back in time, to a slower-paced era when marketing was a social event and the most anticipated outing of the week.

For information about Seattle Farmers call Earth at Save (206-443-1615) or visit them on the web at www.earthsave.org. A complete list of farmer's markets in Washington can be found at www.wafarmers markets.com. For a copy of the state's farmer's market guide with seasons, times and contact numbers, call the Washington State Farmer's Market Association (206-706-1932).

Skate Away *the* Day
ICE AND ROLLER RINKS

Is your family intent on rolling, gliding or sliding the hours away? No problem! Seattle offers a number of great venues for ice, roller and in-line skating, in addition to playing hockey. There are two major ice arenas in the Seattle area, Highland Ice Arena in Shoreline and Sno-King Ice Arena in Lynnwood. Both are open year-round and offer fairly inexpensive public skating sessions along with a full schedule of figure skating, ice dancing and hockey programs. Birthday parties welcomed. If you are a cold weather ice skater, check out the temporary rinks set up during the winter holidays at Seattle Center, Bellevue Downtown Park and Kent's Russell Road Park. With a decidedly festive feel, these rinks hearken back to frozen pond skating. For phone numbers of Seattle area rinks, look in the yellow pages under the heading "Skating Rinks and Instruction."

As for roller-skating, the list is longer and the options for family participation broader. Most

Seattle area roller rinks offer drop-in skate lessons, special family skate sessions and rates, as well as rink time designated just for tots. Birthday parties are always welcome. Southgate Roller Rink in West Seattle is the closest to downtown, but there are also rinks in Lynnwood (Roll-a-Way Skate Center) and in Bellevue (Skate King). Bring your own skates or rent a pair at a cost of under $5. For a full list of Washington roller skating rinks, go online to www.rollerskating.org/rinks/washington.html.

If in-line skating is more your family's style, area roller-rinks allow in-line skates on the floor—as long as they have never been worn outside. Better yet, head to Green Lake (page 170) where the path is divided between those with wheels and those without.

HIGHLAND ICE ARENA
18005 Aurora N., Shoreline
(206) 546-2431

ROLL-A-WAY SKATE CENTER
6210 - 200th S.W., Lynnwood
(425) 778-4446

SKATE KING
2301 - 140th N.E., Bellevue
(425) 641-2046

SNO-KING ICE ARENA
19803 - 68th Ave. W., Lynnwood
(425) 775-7511

SOUTHGATE ROLLER RINK
9646 - 17th Ave. S.W., West Seattle
(206) 762-4030

Places to Paint
YOUR OWN POTTERY

I f your kids need a new medium for expressing their artistic ability, take them to a ceramics studio to paint pottery. You can purchase cups, bowls, piggy banks, vases, picture frames and other assorted knickknacks. The studio supplies the paint, brushes, stencils, sponges and helpful hints to keep your kids busy creating masterpieces. Some studios charge by the hour in addition to the cost of the items, which start at about $5. Younger children tend to finish their projects quickly, so it's a good idea to put a limit on the number of pieces they can paint or this activity will become expensive.

Paint-your-own-pottery studios are also a great idea for birthday parties and field trips. Some studios have separate rooms that can be reserved for groups. When you've finished your art, the studio will have the pieces glazed and fired in about a week. For a studio near you, check the phone book under "Ceramics." One well-established business, Paint the Town, has convenient locations in two shopping centers. Another, City Ceramics, is centrally located on Seattle's Capitol Hill.

CITY CERAMICS
413 – 15th Ave. E., Seattle
(206) 329-1604

PAINT THE TOWN
4527 University Village Court N.E., Seattle (206) 527-8554
7329 – 164th Ave. N.E., Redmond (425) 861-8388

Cool Places to Play
SWIMMING POOLS

The best place to cool off on a hot summer day (or warm up on a dreary winter day) is at your local pool. Community pools (indoor and outdoor) offer swimming lessons for children of all ages. Other aquatic sports and lifesaving instruction are also frequently available. Many pools have swimming sessions for families, classes for parents and tots and special events for kids. Some pools have party rooms to rent for birthday parties.

Seattle Parks and Recreation (206-684-4075; www.cityofseattle.net/parks) has eight indoor pools and two outdoor pools (open summers only). In summer, two dozen wading pools at parks, playgrounds and community centers are open when the weather is warm (above 70 degrees). Call the wading pool hotline (206-684-7796) for details. Lifeguards supervise city beaches and free swimming lessons are offered.

King County (206-296-4232; www.metrokc.gov/parks) operates 15 indoor pools and two outdoor pools (open summers only). King County's Aquatic Center in Federal Way features two pools: one for recreation and the other for competitions. The city of Issaquah's Julius Boehm Pool (50 S.E. Clark St.; 425-837-3350) offers family "Dive-In Movie Nights" throughout the year—movies are free with pool admission.

Other City Pools

BELLEVUE AQUATIC CENTER
601 – 143rd Ave. N.E., Bellevue
(425) 452-4444

LYNNWOOD RECREATION CENTER
18900 – 44th Ave. W., Lynnwood
(425) 771-4030

MOUNTLAKE TERRACE POOL
5303 – 228th St. S.W., Mountlake Terrace
(425) 776-9173

SHORELINE POOL
19030 – 1st Ave. N.E., Shoreline
(206) 362-1307

CHAPTER 4

PLACES TO PLAY

Introduction

Kids are always ready to play. So it's no surprise that Seattle, one of the nation's "most livable cities," is chock-full of places that offer unique ways to play all day long. Enchanted Parks is one of the region's multi-faceted amusement parks and has rides for tots, teens and adults too. For a fun and free summer outing, head to the International Fountain at Seattle Center and let youngsters enjoy a colorful, musical splash.

Need to burn off a little steam? Try a climbing wall or visit The Summit at Snoqualmie for skiing in winter and hiking in summer. You can also take the family golfing, to the arcade or head outdoors to Point Defiance Park. There are tons of great swimming beaches in the area, as well as a fabulous old-fashioned amusement park right in the heart of Seattle. Many of these places are more than happy to make your child's birthday something special. Be sure to call ahead and ask about group rates and special amenities.

NOTE

Find more great places to play outdoors in Chapter 8, as well as at these sites covered elsewhere in this guide:

Two for One Amusements
ENCHANTED PARKS

36201 Enchanted Pkwy. S., Federal Way
(253) 661-8000
www.wildwaves.com

Enchanted Parks is actually two side-by-side attractions. Enchanted Village is a traditional amusement park with rides, entertainment and carnival games. Right next door is Wild Waves, offering adventure-seekers an array of water rides.

There are about two dozen rides at Enchanted Village with many geared to young children and vertigo-prone adults, including a relaxing train ride and antique carousel. Besides the rides, kids will enjoy the big playground, wading pool, puppet shows and other stage shows. For the more daring, there's the triple corkscrew Wild Thing roller coaster.

Wild Waves features a deluge of water slides, river rides and a 24,000 square-foot wave pool. If you have tots in tow, visit the Kids Splash Area complete with a mini river ride, small water slides and a wading pool. The rest of the attractions are best for older kids, as most require riders to be at least 42 inches tall. Plan to come early or on a weekday when it's less crowded.

It's a good idea to bring a change of clothing. Pack a lunch to eat at Enchanted Village; but no food is allowed in Wild Waves Park.

SEASONS AND TIMES
➤ Summer: Daily. Call for exact times. Enchanted Parks is open some weekends in spring and fall.

COST
➤ Enchanted Village: Adults $15, children $12. Enchanted Village and Wild Waves: Adults $25, children (under 48 inches) $23. Prices subject to change. Call in advance to confirm.

GETTING THERE
➤ By car, from Seattle Center, head east on Mercer St. to I-5 South. Take Exit 142-B off I-5 S. and head west. Turn south at the first stoplight onto Enchanted Pkwy. S. Go approximately 1 mile. There are signs to the parking lot. About 40 minutes from Seattle Center.
➤ By public transit, take Metro bus 174, 176, 177, 178, 194 or 195 to the Federal Way Transit Center, than transfer to Pierce Transit bus 402 to Enchanted Village/Wild Waves. Call Metro Transit for route and schedule information (206) 553-3000, or Pierce Transit (800) 562-8109.

NEARBY
➤ Puyallup Fairgrounds.

A *Carnival in the City*
FUN FOREST
AMUSEMENT PARK

Seattle Center, Seattle
(206) 728-1585
www.funforest.com

With so much to see in Seattle Center (page 31), it's hard to know what to visit first. If you're traveling with kids, Fun Forest Amusement Park should top your list. Here, your family can ride on the Ferris wheel for a fine aerial view of the city. Then take a short trip down the Wild River ride, which is always a splash with kids. For the younger set there's Kiddyland, complete with mini bumper cars, a roller coaster and a merry-go-round. Older children enjoy the Windstorm roller coaster and pirate ship ride.

The carnival-like setting comes with all the trimmings—cotton candy, roving entertainers and a midway filled with skill-testing games. Explore the Entertainment Pavilion after you've had your fill outdoors. It offers laser tag, video games, an electronic shooting gallery and miniature golf. Fun Forest's location makes it an easy outing that will have the kids asking for more. This is also a great place to host a birthday party. Call the number above for details.

SEASONS AND TIMES
➤ Outdoor attractions: June—Labor Day, daily, noon—11 pm; Labor Day—May, Fri, 7 pm—11 pm; Sat, noon—11 pm; Sun, noon—8 pm (weather dependent). Indoor Entertainment Pavilion: Year-round, daily, Sun—Thu, 11 am—6 pm; Fri—Sat, 11 am—10 pm.

COST
➤ Rides and attractions vary in cost, each requiring a number of tickets. Books of tickets cost $6 to $15.

GETTING THERE
➤ By car, from I-5 take the Mercer St. Exit and head west towards the Space Needle. Some free parking is available on nearby streets. During special events, parking fees at Center parking lots are based on the number of people in the vehicle (discounts for 2 or more). Expect to pay from $6 to $12 for all-day parking.
➤ By public transit, more than a dozen Metro bus routes service Seattle Center. Festival shuttles run from several suburban Park & Ride lots during special events. Call Metro Transit for route and schedule information (206) 553-3000. Or ride the monorail that travels between Seattle Center and downtown Seattle's Westlake Center.

NEARBY
➤ Space Needle, Pacific Science Center, Children's Museum, Seattle Children's Theatre, International Fountain, Experience Music Project.

COMMENT
➤ Plan a 1-hour visit.

SIMILAR ATTRACTIONS
➤ **Chuck E. Cheese** · 2239 – 148th Ave. N.E., Bellevue (425) 746-5000; 25817 – 104th Ave. S.E., Kent (253) 813-9000; 3717 – 196th Ave. S.W., Lynnwood (425) 778-6566 www.chuckecheese.com

➤ **Funtasia Family Fun Park** · 7212 – 220th St. S.W., Edmonds (425) 775-2174 www.familyfunpark.com

➤ **Tukwila Family Fun Center** · 7300 Fun Center Way, Tukwila (425) 228-7300.

Virtual Playground
GAMEWORKS

1511 - 7th Ave., Seattle
(206) 521-0952

ameWorks is a high-tech heaven featuring the latest and greatest in electronic games spread over 30,000 square feet. Parents can challenge their kids in the multi-player Indy 500 or play traditional arcade games. GameWorks boasts a slew of virtual reality games for the whole family, including a roller coaster, a Jurassic Park mini-theatre ride and snowboarding and jet-skiing games. Conquer your fear of heights at Vertical Reality, the three-story free fall virtual reality ride.

Concerned about your kids playing violent games? GameWorks sells a V-game card that restricts play on about 15 percent of the activities that are considered violent. A caution: set a spending limit before you visit GameWorks. It's easy to spend a lot of money here in a short period of time.

SEASONS AND TIMES
➤ Year-round: Mon—Thu, 11 am—midnight; Fri, 11 am—1 am; Sat, 10 am—1 am; Sun, 11 am—midnight. No one under 18 years after 10 pm.

COST
➤ Admission is free. Games vary from $0.50 to $3. Prepaid game cards are inserted into each game (price is deducted). Discounts and specials available. Mon—Thu, $25 for unlimited play for 2 hours per day. Thursday after 4 pm, 2 for 1 game cards.

GETTING THERE

➤ By car, from south side of Seattle Center, go south on 5th Ave. to Olive Way, turn east and continue to 7th Ave. then turn south. Parking lots nearby (expect to pay $3 per hour or more); metered street parking is sometimes available. About 5 minutes from Seattle Center.

➤ By public transit, take Metro bus 16 south on 3rd Ave. to Pike St. then walk 4 blocks to 7th Ave. Call Metro Transit for route and schedule information (206) 553-3000. Or ride the monorail from Seattle Center to Westlake Center then walk east on Pine St. to 7th Ave. GameWorks is 1 block south.

NEARBY

➤ Seattle Center, Planet Hollywood, downtown shopping district, Pike Place Market.

COMMENT

➤ Plan a 1- to 2-hour visit.

Tee Time
INTERBAY FAMILY GOLF CENTER

2501 – 15th Ave. W., Seattle
(206) 285-2200
www.familygolf.com

B elieve it or not, this rolling green golf course was once a garbage dump. It has been transformed into a beautiful facility where locals and tourists can practice their swing. Whether you play pitch-and-putt or take the kids with you for a 9-hole game, Interbay offers a perfect low-key, low-stress atmosphere. Children are always welcome and the other players are friendly towards them.

No golf pros in your family? Try playing miniature golf instead. The course is a blast and even challenges seasoned players. Don't worry too much about tee times at Interbay, the course has expansive hours and is well lit for play at night. A huge two-story driving range is a great way to hone the skills of even the tiniest golfers. Classes are available for all levels and all ages.

SEASONS AND TIMES
➤ Year-round: Daily, Mon—Sat, 7 am—11 pm; Sun, 7 am—10 pm.

COST
➤ Less than $10 per person. Equipment rental extra.

GETTING THERE
➤ By car, from south side of Seattle Center, turn west on Denny Way and follow it as it curves north and becomes Western Ave. W., then Elliott Ave. W. and finally 15th Ave. W. The course will be on the west side of the road. Free parking on site. About 6 minutes from Seattle Center.
➤ By public transit, take Metro bus 17 north on 3rd Ave. Call Metro Transit for route and schedule information (206) 553-3000.

COMMENT
➤ Plan a 1- to 2-hour visit.

SIMILAR ATTRACTIONS
➤ **Jefferson Park Learning Center** · 4101 Beacon S., Seattle (206) 763-8989.

➤ **Kent Family Golf Center** · 9116 S. 212th St., Kent (253) 850-8300.

➤ **Puetz Golf Superstore (driving range)** · 11762 Aurora Ave. N., Seattle (206) 362-2272.

Liquid Lights
INTERNATIONAL
FOUNTAIN

Seattle Center, Seattle
(206) 684-7200
www.seattlecenter.com

I n most cities, you get in trouble for putting your feet in public fountains. At the International Fountain in Seattle Center, however, youngsters are encouraged to play in the water. With its musically synchronized rays of colorful water shooting in every direction, the fountain is more than art. Recently, Seattle Center officials redesigned the structure to make it user-friendly, building ramps to make it easier for kids to reach the water sprays.

To make the most of your visit, pack a picnic and lunch by the edge of the fountain. On warm spring days and in the summer, it's difficult to tear your children away. Bring a towel and a change of clothes for everyone. Later, steer the gang to nearby Fun Forest (page 79) or one of the other attractions at Seattle Center (page 31).

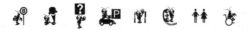

SEASONS AND TIMES
➜ Year-round: Daily.

COST
➜ Free.

GETTING THERE

➤ By car, from I-5, take the Mercer St. Exit and head west towards the Space Needle. Some free parking is available on nearby streets. During special events, parking fees at Center parking lots are based on number of people in vehicle (discounts for 2 or more). Expect to pay from $6 to $12 for all-day parking.

➤ By public transit, more than a dozen Metro bus routes service Seattle Center. Festival shuttles run from several suburban Park & Ride lots during special events. Call Metro Transit for route and schedule information (206) 553-3000. Or ride the monorail that travels between Seattle Center and downtown Seattle's Westlake Center.

NEARBY

➤ Fun Forest, Space Needle, Monorail, Pacific Science Center, Children's Museum, Seattle Children's Theatre.

Sand, Sun and Waves
LAKE AND SOUND BEACHES

With Puget Sound, Lake Washington and numerous other lakes, greater Seattle is home to an unbelievable number of beautiful swimming beaches. The water can be cold, especially in Puget Sound, but youngsters don't seem to mind. In summer, lifeguards are on duty at most beaches. Free swimming lessons are offered at Seattle's Lake Washington beaches. Many saltwater beaches have great tide pools and are perfect for beachcombing. You can read about another popular beach, Alki Beach, in Chapter 1. For even more beaches, see Chapter 8 of this guide.

LAKE WASHINGTON BEACHES

Seattle Beaches
(206) 684-4075

Parks have changing facilities and picnic tables. Some have playgrounds, sports courts and other recreation. Free swimming lessons for ages six and up by pre-registration.

MADISON PARK
2300 – 43rd Ave. E.

MADRONA PARK
853 Lake Washington Blvd.

MATHEWS BEACH PARK
Sand Point Way N.E. and N.E. 93rd St.

MOUNT BAKER PARK
2521 Lake Park Dr. S.

PRITCHARD BEACH PARK
8400 – 55th Ave. S.

Kirkland Beaches
(425) 828-1217

Picnic areas, playgrounds and changing facilities.

HOUGHTON BEACH
5811 Lake Washington Blvd.

WAVERLY BEACH
633 Waverly Park Way

JUANITA BEACH PARK
9703 Juanita Dr. N.E. (206) 296-4232

O. O. DENNY PARK
12032 Holmes Point Dr. N.E., Juanita (206) 296-4232

Bellevue Beaches
(425) 452-6881

CHISM BEACH PARK
1175 – 96th Ave. S.E.

CLYDE BEACH PARK
2 – 92nd Ave. N.E.

ENATAI BEACH PARK
3519 – 108th Ave. S.E.

MEYDENBAUER BEACH PARK
419 – 98th Ave. N.E.

NEWCASTLE BEACH PARK
4400 Lake Washington Blvd. S.

PUGET SOUND BEACHES

No lifeguards.

GOLDEN GARDENS PARK
8498 Seaview Pl. N.W., Seattle (206) 684-4075
Sandy beach and small playground.

Edmonds Beaches
(425) 771-0230

OLYMPIC BEACH
Dayton St. and Admiral Way, by fishing pier
Picnic area, fishing, public art.

MARINA BEACH PARK
Admiralty Way S.
Playground, picnic area, kite hill.

UNDERWATER PARK
Brackett's Landing, north of ferry dock
Tide pools, naturalist walks, popular with divers.

DASH POINT STATE PARK
5700 S.W. Dash Point Rd., Federal Way (253) 661-4955
Overnight camping, playground, sandy beach,
picnic areas.

RICHMOND BEACH SALTWATER PARK
2021 N.W. 190th St., Shoreline (206) 546-5041

Playground, beach, picnic areas.

SALTWATER STATE PARK
25205 – 8th Pl. S., Des Moines (253) 661-4956

Overnight camping, beachcombing, picnic facilities, hiking and nature trails.

OTHER LAKES

LAKE SAMMAMISH STATE PARK
20606 S.E. 56th St., Issaquah (425) 455-7010

Sandy beach, swimming, fishing, boating, picnic facilities, playground.

PINE LAKE PARK
2405 – 228th Ave. S.E., Issaquah (206) 296-4232

Swimming beach, playground, sports fields, picnic facilities.

LAKE WILDERNESS PARK
22500 S.E. 248th St., Maple Valley (206) 296-4232

Community center, play area, swimming beach, sports fields, walking paths, fishing pier, picnic facilities.

LAKE MERIDIAN PARK
14800 S.E. 272nd St., Kent (253) 856-5100

Large playground, swimming beach, fishing, boating, picnic facilities.

ANGLE LAKE PARK
19408 International Blvd., SeaTac (206) 439-9273

Swimming, boat launch, fishing, recreation areas, picnic facilities.

LAKE BALLINGER PARK
23000 Lakeview Dr., Mountlake Terrace (425) 776-9173

Swimming, fishing, boating, playground, picnicking, athletic fields.

Play All Day at
POINT DEFIANCE PARK

5400 N. Pearl St., Tacoma
(253) 305-1000

Point Defiance Park is perfect for families looking for fun and adventure. Make your first stop Never Never Land, where kids can step into their favorite nursery rhymes. There are more than 30 walk-though exhibits with characters from all their favorite stories including *Goldilocks and the Three Bears*, *Humpty Dumpty* and *Little Bo Peep*. It's a magical spot for a birthday party. Often, live entertainment and special events—such as egg hunts—are featured.

Fort Nisqually welcomes you to visit another era. This reconstructed fur trading and farming post was originally established in the 1800s. The Fort hosts several living history events during the year, when youngsters can meet historical figures. If your brood want to ride the rails, head to Camp 6 Logging Museum and hop aboard a steam train that travels through the woods. A special Santa Train operates in December. Don't miss the museum's exhibits. They highlight Washington's early logging days.

The park boasts other attractions, including Point Defiance Zoo & Aquarium (page 150) and seven formal gardens (including a Japanese Garden and a Rose Garden). In summer, the beach is a big draw. Boat rentals are available (at the Boathouse Marina) and there's fishing. Board the ferry for a short ride to Vashon Island, or explore more than 20 miles of forested hiking trails in the park.

SEASONS AND TIMES

➤ Park: Year-round, dawn—dusk. Never Never Land: Memorial Day—Labor Day, Wed—Sun, 11 am—6 pm. Fort Nisqually: June—Aug, daily, 11 am—6 pm; Sept—Oct and Apr—May, Sat—Sun, 11 am—5 pm. Other times for special events. Camp 6 Logging Museum: Outdoor exhibits, year-round, dawn—dusk; indoor exhibits, Apr—Oct, Wed—Sun, 10 am—4 pm. Train rides: Apr—Sept, Sat—Sun, starting at noon. Santa Train first 3 weekends in Dec.

COST

➤ Park admission free. Nominal fees are charged at some attractions.

GETTING THERE

➤ By car, from Seattle Center, head east on Mercer St. to I-5 South. Follow 1-5 S. to Exit 132. Go west and follow the signs to Hwy. 16 W. (Bremerton/Gig Harbor). Take the 6th Ave. Exit and turn west. Turn north onto Pearl St. It dead-ends at Point Defiance Park. About 50 minutes from Seattle.

NEARBY

➤ Washington State History Museum.

COMMENT

➤ Pack a lunch and plan to visit for the day.

Ascent to the Sky
ROCK CLIMBING

Looking for fitness fun for the whole family? Try one of Seattle's three major rock climbing facilities, where you'll learn the tricks of the sport on craggy indoor and outdoor climbing walls. Stone Gardens, Vertical World and the REI Climbing Wall offer well-designed indoor facilities and the staff is knowledgeable. For more of a challenge, head to the outdoor walls at Stone Gardens and Vertical World. Both facilities offer classes for climbers of all ages and abilities, complete with expert instructors and belay teams. Call ahead to find out about special events and party packages.

Stone Gardens
2839 N.W. Market St., Seattle
(206) 781-9828
www.stonegardens.com

Kids Climb is an excellent way for those 6 to 16 to learn to climb. The Junior Climbing Program offers group classes to help youngsters improve skills, fitness and mental awareness. There's even a junior competitive climbing team. Bring the family for free clinics on Thursdays at 7 pm.

➛ Wall: Mon, Wed, Fri–Sat, 10 am–10 pm; Tue, Thu, 6 am–11 pm; Sun, 10 am–7 pm. Kids Climb: Mon, Fri, 5 pm–7 pm; Sat, 10 am–noon. Junior Climbers: Mon, Wed, Sun, 5 pm–7 pm.

➛ Wall (per day): Adults $12, youths (under 17) $10. Kids Climb: $24 per child. Junior Climbers (per month): Members $45, non-members $65. Equipment rental extra. Memberships available.

REI Climbing Wall

222 Yale Ave. N., Seattle
(206) 223-1944
www.rei.com

The REI wall does not offer classes. An expert belay team is ready and willing to assist you and offer tips as you scale the giant obelisk.

➤ Mon, Wed—Fri, 10 am—7 pm; Sat, 10 am—4 pm; Sun, 11 am—3 pm.

➤ $5 per climb.

Vertical World

2123 W. Elmore St., Seattle (206) 283-4497
and 15036-B N.E. 95th St., Redmond (425) 881-8826
www.verticalworld.com

The Level I Introduction to Climbing class offers the basics on rope handling, belaying and technique. Climb Time program for kids aged 6 to 12 features supervised climbing for an hour and a half. The Parent Belay program provides adults with tips on how to belay their children.

➤ Mon, Wed, Fri, 10 am—10 pm; Tue, Thu, 6 am—10 pm; Sat—Sun, 10 am—7 pm.

➤ Members $15 to $30, non-members $25 to $40.

Ski, Hike or Climb
THE SUMMIT AT SNOQUALMIE

Snoqualmie Pass, Exit 52-54 off I-90 E.
(425) 434-7669, (206) 236-1600 (Skiers Info),
(888) SNO-INFO (Road Conditions)
www.summit-at-snoqualmie.com

Opportunities for outside recreation abound in the mountains surrounding Seattle. Less than an hour away, the Summit at Snoqualmie offers families seasonal skiing, snowboarding, snowshoeing, tubing, sledding as well as hiking and climbing. Located in the Snoqualmie National Forest, the Summit is at the heart of the Cascade Mountain Range. It features four major ski areas with dozens of runs for day and night downhill skiing and groomed trails for cross-country. Instruction and equipment rental are available. In warmer weather, there's hiking and backpacking on the Summit and its approaches on groomed and not-so-groomed trails. For trail information, visit www.parks.wa.gov

Whether yours is a winter or summer outing, consider joining the Mountaineers Club (800-573-8484), which operates the Mountaineers Lodge at Snoqualmie Pass Summit. The lodge is family-oriented and has its own trails that are rarely crowded. The one-time $35 initiation fee and $90 annual family fee are well worth it if you plan to go several times in winter.

SEASONS AND TIMES
➤ Year-round: Daily.

COST
➤ Varies depending on activity. Hiking trails are free.

GETTING THERE
➤ By car, from Seattle Center, head east on Mercer St. to I-5 South. Take I-5 S. to I-90 E. Follow I-90 for about 35 miles to Snoqualmie Pass. Free parking on site. About 1 hour from Seattle Center.
➤ Several charter and tour bus companies offer service to the Summit. Check the yellow pages for company contact information.

NEARBY
➤ Snoqualmie Falls.

COMMENT
➤ Plan a 3- to 4-hour visit.

SIMILAR ATTRACTIONS
➤ **Stevens Pass** · State Hwy. 2, (206) 812-4510; www.stevenspass.com
➤ **Mt. Baker Ski Area** · State Hwy. 542, (360) 734-6771; www.mtbakerskiarea.com
➤ **Crystal Mountain** · off State Hwy. 410, (888) 754-6199; www.skicrystal.com

Other Places to Play

Playspace

Crossroads Shopping Center
15600 N.E. 8th St., Bellevue
(425) 644-4500

Kids can play all day here, crawling through tunnels, jumping in ball pits and riding a swirly slide. For more fun, check out the dress-up area, play kitchen, train table, blocks, books and more. Drop—off daycare is available for parents shopping in the mall. There's even a "parents night out" package where adults can leave their kids and go listen to free music from 7 pm to 10 pm on Fridays and Saturdays. Birthday parties available.

➛ Year round: Mon—Thu, 10 am—9 pm; Fri—Sat, 10 am—10:30 pm; Sun, 11 am—7 pm.

➛ With parents: $4.50 per child for up to 4 hours. Drop-off: $5.50 per child for first hour. $4 each additional hour up to 4 hours. Parents Night Out: $15 first child, $12 each additional child.

➛ Head east from Seattle Center on Mercer St. to I-5 North. Take I-5 N. to the SR-520 East Exit and continue on SR-520 to the 148th Ave. N.E. South Exit. Proceed on 148th to N.E. 8th St. and turn east. Go to 156th Ave. N.E. and turn north to shopping center.

CHAPTER 5

PLACES
TO LEARN

Introduction

Part of the fun of parenting is satisfying your children's endless curiosity about the world around them. In the Seattle area, there are plenty of interesting sites where you can do just that. See where the huge Boeing 747 and 777s are made at the Everett Boeing Factory. Experience Native American culture and food at Tillicum Village on Blake Island, or head across the Sound to the Bremerton Naval Museum and Poulsbo Marine Science Center. Interactive exhibits teach kids about regional history at the Washington State History Museum and maritime activities are highlighted at Odyssey, the Maritime Discovery Center.

For art buffs, the Bellevue Art Museum is the place "to see, explore and make art." Learn about nature at Camp Long in West Seattle, the only place in the city with overnight camping. At the Center for Wooden Boats, take a free ride on a classic wooden boat Sunday afternoons. Finally, don't miss the awe-inspiring natural wonder of Snoqualmie Falls, a sacred place to Native Americans and one of the top tourist destinations in the area.

Art for All Ages
BELLEVUE ART MUSEUM

510 Bellevue Way N.E., Bellevue
(425) 519-0770; (425) 454-3322 (school)
www.bellevueart.org

At the Bellevue Art Museum (BAM), art starts on the outside. The architectural design of the building by Steven Holl provides inspiration for many of the theme exhibitions inside. After your kids have ogled the outside, head indoors to explore and make your own art.

The Explore Gallery allows visitors to examine architectural tools up close. You can try your hand at designing a room using digital camera technology. You'll even get to complete a 30-second video. BAM has many stimulating exhibits. At Luminous, kids see their image reflected in a single drop of water. Also on display are nine water-dispensing vending machines, their front panels creating one panoramic photo of Niagara Falls. If tradition is more to your liking, there's plenty of art on the walls with reader cards beside each piece.

To get the most from your visit, keep an eye out for the Art Cart. It features hands-on activities relating to the art on display at the gallery. BAM also operates an arts school that offers 35 different classes. Check out the ceramics class created just for families.

SEASONS AND TIMES
➤ Year-round: Tue, Sat, 10 am–5 pm; Wed–Fri, noon–8 pm; Sun, noon–5 pm.

COST
➤ Adults $6, seniors (over 62) and students (6 to 18) $4, under 6 free. Free on 3rd Thursday of each month.

GETTING THERE
➤ By car, from Seattle Center, head east on Mercer St. and take I-5 North. Follow I-5 N. to SR-520 and head east on SR-520. Take the Bellevue Way Exit and proceed south to N.E. 6th St. Parking available in lots. About 20 minutes from Seattle Center.
➤ By public transit, take Sound Transit 550 from downtown Seattle bus tunnel to Bellevue Transit Center. Walk 2 blocks west on N.E. 6th St. to the museum. Call Metro Transit for route and schedule information (206) 553-3000.

NEARBY
➤ Bellevue Square, Bellevue Downtown Park, Meydenbauer Park, Lake Washington, Kirkland waterfront.

COMMENT
➤ Plan a 1- to 2-hour visit.

Take to the Skies
BOEING EVERETT
FACTORY TOUR

3003 W. Casino Rd., Everett
(800) 464-1476

For a fascinating look at how commercial jets are manufactured, head to the Boeing Everett Plant. The facility is enormous—big enough to hold 75 football fields. The building is the largest in the world by volume according to the Guinness Book of World Records. And it needs to be. It's the place where the biggest commercial jets (747, 767 and 777s) are made.

The hour-long tour begins with a video about the plane's production process. You'll learn interesting facts such as it takes a million parts and over six months to build a single plane. Next you'll walk up a flight of stairs to look down at the production line and see planes in various stages of assembly and testing. Kids love the huge cranes that move the airplane parts high in the air. The tour concludes with a bus ride to Paine Field and a look at the finished products on the runway.

Safety and security are important. Kids must be at least four feet two inches tall to participate in the tour. Also, you cannot bring hand-held items including cameras, purses, cellular phones or notepads.

SEASONS AND TIMES
→ Year-round: Mon—Fri, hourly between 9 am—11 am, 1 pm—3 pm. Closed most holidays and in late Dec.

COST
→ Adults $5, seniors (over 62) and children (under 16) $3. Tickets are first come/first served and often sell-out in summer months. Sales begin at 8:30 am each day. For ticket availability inquiries on the day of tour call (425) 342-8500. Tickets may also be reserved 24 hours or more in advance for $10/person (call 800-464-1476).

GETTING THERE
→ By car, from Seattle Center go east on Mercer St. to I-5 North. Take I-5 N. to Exit 189 and head west on State Hwy. 526. Continue for about 3 1/2 miles and then follow the signs to the Tour Center.

About 40 minutes from Seattle Center.
➤ Public transportation is limited. Call Metro Transit for route and schedule information (206) 553-3000.

NEARBY
➤ Forest Park Animal Farm.

COMMENT
➤ Restrooms available before and after tour, but not during. Call ahead if you are bringing a wheelchair.

Ahoy Matey!
BREMERTON NAVAL MUSEUM

130 Washington St., Bremerton
(360) 479-7447

If you've got a child who loves war ships, submarines and other vessels of the U.S. Navy, you can't miss with a trip to Bremerton Naval Museum. The museum showcases a wide variety of naval artifacts including models of ships, from modern vessels to World War II and earlier. Explore the shipyard where boats are built and serviced. Kids can try their hand at steering a great Navy ship on a simulated bridge deck overlooking Puget Sound. This is not as hands-on as many of the Seattle's other museums, but it is one of the best places to learn about naval history in the country. Allow for a 45-minute ferry ride from Seattle's Waterfront to the museum.

SEASONS AND TIMES
➜ Summer (Mar—Nov): Mon—Sat, 10 am—5 pm; Sun, 1 pm—5 pm.
Winter (Dec—Feb): Tue—Sat, 10 am—4 pm; Sun, 1 pm—5 pm.

COST
➜ Suggestion donation $1.

GETTING THERE
➜ By car, from east side of Seattle Center, follow Broad St. west
towards Puget Sound. Turn south onto Alaskan Way and follow
Alaskan to Colman Dock Ferry Terminal at the south end of the
Waterfront. Take the Bremerton Ferry (walk on is less costly). The
museum is on Washington St., half a block from the ferry terminal.
About a 5-minute drive to Waterfront terminal and 45 minute ferry
ride.
➜ By public transit, board any southbound bus on 2nd St. and ride
to Madison St. Walk 1 block west to Waterfront and ferry terminal.
Call Metro Transit for route and schedule information (206) 553-
3000.

COMMENT
➜ Plan a 1- to 2-hour visit.

SIMILAR ATTRACTIONS
➜ **Naval Undersea Museum** · Learn about marine science, naval
history, and evolving undersea technology. See dive suits, torpe-
does and the submersible that helped explore the Titanic. 610
Dowell St., in Keyport (360) 396-4148 http://num.kpt.nuwc.navy.mil

➜ **USS *Turner Joy* Tour** · Tour a naval destroyer and floating
museum of the Vietnam War-era Navy. Bremerton Waterfront
(360) 792-2457.

➜ **Naval Shipyard Mothball Fleet Harbor Tour** · Narrated
historical tour. Weekends in spring and daily from May to
September. Boardwalk (360) 377-8924.

Roughing It in the City
CAMP LONG

**5200 – 35th Ave. S.W., Seattle
(206) 684-7434
www.cityofseattle.net/parks/Environment/camplong.htm**

Seattle's only urban campground was built on part of the West Seattle Golf Course in the late 1930s. Workers from the Works Progress Administration used recycled paving blocks and lumber from other projects and planted ornamental trees from a bankrupt nursery. Since its completion, organized groups have been using it for camping expeditions.

In 1984, Camp Long opened to the public and now hosts natural history and environmental education programs throughout the year. During the day, your family can check out the 20-foot Schurman Rock climbing structure, or the "Glacier," a series of rock slopes made to scale. There are plenty of hiking trails too, including a half-mile nature trail that's great for kids. For more fun, camp overnight at one of the rustic cabins, equipped with double bunk beds and sleeping up to 12.

Camp Long offers a full slate of nature programs, including free naturalist-led walks on weekends. Tot walks are held once a month; art and nature are integrated into craft classes; holidays are celebrated with special programs; and off-site field trips are organized occasionally. Nocturnal Naturalist programs are popular with overnight campers and anyone who enjoys learning about astronomy, wildlife and nature lore. Naturalists lead the adventurous on nighttime explorations including tide pooling, night hikes, hayrides and stargazing.

SEASONS AND TIMES
→ Lodge: Tue—Sun, 8:30 am—5 pm (evening programs on weekends). Check-in for overnight camping: 2:30 pm—4:45 pm. Gate closes at 10 pm for campers.

COST
→ Park: Free. Fees for some classes and activities. Overnight camping: $35 per cabin (reservations required).

GETTING THERE
→ By car, from Seattle Center head east on Mercer St. to I-5 South. From I-5 S., take Exit 163 Spokane St./West Seattle Bridge and head west. At the first light after crossing the bridge, turn south onto 35th Ave. S.W. Go eight-tenths of a mile to Dawson St. and turn east into the park. About 20 minutes from Seattle Center.
→ By public transit, take Metro bus 21 to the corner of 35th Ave. S.W. and S.W. Dawson St. Call Metro Transit for route and schedule information (206) 553-3000.

NEARBY
→ Alki Beach, Log House Museum.

Wooden Flotillas
CENTER FOR WOODEN BOATS

1010 Valley St., Seattle
(206) 382-2628
www.cwb.org

I n a city surrounded by lakes and the Sound, it's not surprising boats are popular. On the first Saturday in May, boats of all sizes parade through the Montlake Cut and into Lake Washington on Boating Day. But you won't have to wait until then to see watercraft because more than 100 wooden vessels are showcased at the Center for Wooden Boats.

First stop by the Boat House, pick up life jackets for your youngsters and check out the model boats and photos on display. Then walk the docks to see the huge boat collection including sailboats, rowboats, yachts, shells, canoes, gillnetters, paddle boats, ocean fishing vessels and more. If you have time, stop in at the shop and see boats being repaired and restored. On Sundays at 2 pm (weather permitting), take a free ride around Lake Union in one of these classics. The Center also rents rowboats and sailboats.

On the Fourth of July weekend, visit the Lake Union Wooden Boat Festival. You can watch boat building contests, yacht races, canoe carving or build your own toy boat. You'll also see more than

100 visiting vessels. The kids' area offers hands-on activities and the Music Stage features sea shanties and other live folk music.

SEASONS AND TIMES
➤ Year-round: Daily, 11 am–5 pm (closed Tue in winter)

COST
➤ Free, donations welcome.

GETTING THERE
➤ By car, from Seattle Center go east on Mercer St. to Westlake Ave. and turn north. Go to Valley St., then turn east. About 3 minutes from Seattle Center.
➤ By public transit, take northbound Metro bus 26 or 28 from 4th Ave. Get off at Mercer. Walk 1 block north to Valley and 3 blocks east to the Boat Center. Call Metro Transit for route and schedule information (206) 553-3000.
➤ On foot, follow car directions.

NEARBY
➤ Lake Union, Gas Works Park, Seattle Center.

COMMENT
➤ Plan a 1-to 2-hour visit.

O Captain, My Captain
ODYSSEY, THE MARITIME DISCOVERY CENTER

Alaskan Way, Pier 66, Seattle
(206) 374-4000
www.ody.org

Maritime trade and industry have made a major mark on this port city. Through the 40 exhibits at Odyssey, The Maritime Discovery Center families learn about Puget Sound's diverse natural water habitat. They see how Seattle residents share the resource for commercial and recreational uses.

In the Sharing the Sound Gallery, kids use simulation technology to navigate a ship through Elliott Bay or paddle a kayak through the inlets of Puget Sound. For a lesson in simplicity, visit the Harbor Watch Gallery. Here visitors look out at the waterway through a huge window and try their hand at vessel identification. The gallery's Inside Ship display will help you distinguish between the types of ships. Kids have a blast trying to use a crane to lift and deposit ship containers.

For smaller children, the Harvesting the Sea Gallery lets them explore an authentic small-scale fishing vessel. Finally the Ocean Trade Gallery explains ship trade with other countries. It also offers a great lesson in the physics of propulsion by inviting visitors to pedal a full-sized ship propeller.

The center offers special events throughout the year, including Marine Career Day in March.

SEASONS AND TIMES
➤ Year-round: Tue—Sat, 10 am—5 pm; Sun, noon—5 pm. Closed Mondays and most holidays.

COST
➤ Adults $6.75, seniors (over 62) and students (5 to 18) $4.50, under 5 free.

GETTING THERE
➤ By car, from the east side of Seattle Center, take Broad St. west towards Puget Sound. Turn south onto Alaskan Way. Odyssey is 4 piers down on the waterfront side. Limited metered parking along Alaskan Way. About 5 minutes from Seattle Center.
➤ By public transit, walk from Seattle Center to the waterfront via Broad St. Take the Waterfront Street Car Route 99 to Odyssey, midway along the waterfront. Or, take any bus heading south on 1st Ave. and walk down the Harbor Steps or Pike Place Market steps to Western Ave. and Waterfront and head north to Odyssey. Call Metro Transit for route and schedule information (206) 553-3000.

NEARBY
➤ Waterfront, Pike Place Market, Seattle Center, Myrtle Edwards Park, Washington State Ferries.

COMMENT
➤ Plan at least a 1-hour visit.

Underwater at the Sound
POULSBO MARINE
SCIENCE CENTER

18743 Front St. N.E., Poulsbo
(360) 779-5549
www.poulsbomsc.org

Visit the many ship and shipping-oriented museums to learn about how Puget Sound has been used for commerce, military protection and as a center for Pacific Ocean fisheries. At Poulsbo Marine Science Center however, you'll learn the submerged story of Puget Sound. The center is dedicated to the preservation of the Northwest's marine environment and seeks to educate visitors about making ecologically-wise choices when it comes to living, working and playing on the Sound.

This hands-on learning center offers something for the entire family. Packed with interesting plants and animals from Puget Sound, kids get a chance to get their hands wet by exploring different aspects of sea life in special "touch trays." They get up-close-and-personal with sea cucumbers, starfish, clams, urchins, snails and a giant Pacific octopus. The skeleton of a gray whale that washed up on the shores of a local beach gives an educational glimpse into the marine life of the Sound. The center offers a wide variety of classes throughout the year, all geared toward children and families. Got a birthday coming? Consider a marine-theme party at the center.

SEASONS AND TIMES
➤ Year-round: Daily, 11 am—5 pm. Closed Dec 24, 25, 31, New Year's and Thanksgiving. Last admission 4:30 pm.

COST
➤ Adults $4, seniors (over 64), students (13 to 17) and active duty military $3, children (2 to 12) $2, under 2 free.

GETTING THERE
➤ By car, from east side of Seattle Center, go west on Broad St. toward Puget Sound. Turn south onto Alaskan Way and follow Alaskan to Colman Dock Ferry Terminal at south end of Waterfront. Take Winslow ferry and stay on Highway 305 coming off ferry. Cross the Agate Pass Bridge and continue to follow Hwy. 305 to intersection with Hostmark St. Turn west onto Hostmark. It will curve northwest to become Front St. Follow Front toward the waterfront. About 5 minutes to ferry terminal, 30 minutes on ferry, 20-minute drive to museum.

NEARBY
➤ Poulsbo, Winslow, Bainbridge Island Ferry.

COMMENT
➤ Plan to visit for an hour or more.

Spiritual Waters
SNOQUALMIE
FALLS/SALISH LODGE

6501 Railroad Ave., Snoqualmie
(425) 888-2556 or (800) 826-6124
www.salishlodge.com or www.ci.snoqualmie.wa.us

L ocated on Snoqualmie River high in the Cascade Mountains, Snoqualmie Falls is considered one of the Native peoples' most sacred places. According to Snoqualmie Chief Ernie Barr, it's a place "where Heaven and Earth meet."

Before the land became a tourist destination, Native Americans would meet at the falls to trade goods and camp in winter. However, when the railroad reached the area in 1889, the majestic falls became a hot attraction. Currently there is a huge hydroelectric plant stunningly situated on the cusp of the falls and a swanky hotel luring 1.5 million visitors to the falls each year.

The conflict between Natives and the electric plant operators—who wanted to slow or cut off the cascading waters for portions of the year—provides a lesson in history for families. While viewing this natural wonder, kids learn about the waterfall's importance to the Natives, as well as how the dam supplies energy to the Seattle area. A wide observation deck provides incredible views of the falling water. Follow the winding trail alongside the waterfall for spectacular vistas narrated by display panels. If you get thirsty looking at the water, head to the Salish for a snack. Seeing the beauty and majesty of the falls is well worth the 45-minute drive.

SEASONS AND TIMES
➤ Year-round: Daily, dawn—dusk.

COST
➤ Free.

GETTING THERE
➤ By car, from Seattle Center, head east on Mercer St. to I-5 South. Follow I-5 S. to the I-90 E. Exit and follow I-90 E. to Snoqualmie. Take Exit 25 and head north onto Snoqualmie Pkwy. Continue until you reach the lights on Railroad Ave. Head west on Railroad for 1/4 mile. Look for signs to the lodge and falls viewing area. Parking available on-site. About 45 minutes from Seattle Center.

NEARBY
➤ Northwest Railway Museum, Snoqualmie Valley Railroad, Issaquah, Summit at Snoqualmie Pass.

COMMENT
➤ Plan a 1-hour visit.

Native Lore at
TILLICUM VILLAGE & TOUR

**Piers 55 and 56, Seattle
(206) 443-1244
www.tillicumvillage.com**

Although Tillicum Village Tour on Blake Island is expensive, think of it as investing in your children's introduction to the culture, arts and music of Northwest Native people.

The tour starts at Pier 55 where you board a small private ferry for an eight-mile ride to Blake Island. Once aboard, youngsters enjoy watching the white caps while older kids and adults appreciate the narrated tour. As you approach the island, take a few minutes to absorb its beauty, preserved by its Washington State Park status. With 16 miles of trails, 500 acres of natural forest and 5 miles of beach, Blake Island is a natural paradise.

At Tillicum Village, you first enter a Native American long house. While inside, guests are treated to a traditional alder-smoked salmon meal and a colorful, educational stage production based on Native American culture and lore. Following the meal, there's about an hour left to take in the rest of the island. Kids enjoy learning about the fish smoking process, checking out the gift shop and playing on the beach. To make the most of your visit, inquire about special summer tours that include park exploration and wildlife sighting.

SEASONS AND TIMES
➤ Year-round. Departure times vary by season. Call for details.

COST
➤ Adults $60, seniors (over 59) $54, children (5 to 12) $24, under 5 free.

GETTING THERE
➤ By car, from the east side of Seattle Center go west on Broad St. towards Puget Sound. Turn south on Alaskan Way and proceed to Piers 55 and 56. Some meter parking available under Alaskan Way Viaduct. About 5 minutes from Seattle Center.
➤ By public transit, take Metro bus 10 or 12 along 1st Ave., or any other downtown buses along 2nd or 3rd Ave. Access the waterfront

via Harbor Steps or via the Pike Place Hill climb at Pike Place Market. Call Metro Transit for route and schedule information (206) 553-3000.

NEARBY
➤ Waterfront, Blake Island State Park.

COMMENT
➤ Plan a 4- to 6-hour visit, depending on the tour.

Days of Yore
WASHINGTON STATE HISTORY MUSEUM

1911 Pacific Ave., Tacoma
(253) 272-9747
www.wshs.org/wshm

For a fun and educational glimpse into the history of the Evergreen State, visit the Washington State History Museum. In the Great Hall of Washington History exhibit, the past comes alive. Kids meet explorer William Clark, walk through a traditional Southern Coast Salish plank house, sit in a covered wagon and dress up in pioneer clothes and gold-mining gear. Talking characters illuminate the past—listen in as Mac and Leon discuss the Depression, a basket maker and granddaughter converse about their lives, and Meriweather Lewis speaks to Native Americans at Fort Vancouver.

In Walla Walla's Schwabacher General Store, meet six life-sized characters and hear them talk about their wagon train journey in the 1870s. A display of Native American masks is accompanied by voices describing how the Natives were affected by disease and epidemics brought by explorers. At a computer touch screen, kids can learn Native American words. The cave-in of Roslyn coal mine is so realistically depicted that it may disturb younger children.

For a more relaxed environment, stop in at the three-screen Columbia River Theater and take a ride down the Columbia. The Model Railway display, spanning 1800 square feet is a must for train fans. A modern-day exhibit is also the museum's tallest—a 42-foot electric tower depicts hydroelectric power from the Columbia Basin Project. For more interactive displays, visit the History Lab Learning Center. Before leaving, pick up a unique memento at the Museum's gift shop.

SEASONS AND TIMES
➤ Summer (Apr–Labor Day): Mon–Sat, 10 am–5 pm (Thu until 8 pm); Sun, 11 am–5 pm. Winter (Labor Day–Apr): Same as summer hours but closed Mondays.

COST
➤Adults $7, seniors (over 59) $6.25, students (6 to 17) $5, under 6 free. Free admission on Thu, 5 pm–8 pm.

GETTING THERE
➤ By car, from Seattle Center go east on Mercer St. to I-5 South. Take I-5 S. to Exit 133 (Tacoma City Center). Follow the I-705/City Center signs to 21st St., then turn south onto 21st. Follow it to Pacific Ave. and turn west. Parking lot is behind the museum. About 40 minutes from Seattle Center.

NEARBY

➤ Point Defiance Park, Zoo and Aquarium.

COMMENT

➤ Plan a 1- to 2-hour visit.

SIMILAR ATTRACTIONS

➤ **Washington State Capital Museum** · Exhibits about the state capital and Native American history. 211 W. 21st Ave., Olympia (360) 753-2580.

CHAPTER 6

MUSIC, THEATER, DANCE AND CINEMA

Introduction

B e glad you have children. Without them, you might miss a lot of what Seattle has to offer in dance, theater, music and film. In and around the city, there are a growing number of companies committed to providing families with engaging and challenging artistic productions. The Seattle Children's Theatre is known worldwide for its innovative, creative, classic and modern performances. On Mercer Island, Youth Theatre Northwest presents shows created by children, for children. In Kirkland, Studio East offers both student productions and StoryBook Theatre's twisted fairy tales.

Seattle is home to one of the most revered puppet theaters in the country, the Northwest Puppet Center. Thistle Theatre specializes in the Japanese form of bunraku puppetry, taking its shows to communities and schools around town. The Pacific Northwest Ballet and Olympic Ballet ensure family accessibility to top-notch dance, while the Seattle Symphony presents concert series for kids.

For more fun, check out a laser light show, eye-popping magic and giant-screen movies. No matter what you choose to do, the vibrant Seattle arts scene will certainly make you thank the youngster who dragged you there.

Eye-popping Magic at
ILLUSIONZ MAGICAL ENTERTAINMENT CENTER

**1025 N.W. Gilman Blvd., Issaquah
(425) 427-2444
www.Illusionz.com**

To find big time magic with flashy disappearing acts and people being sawed in half, you'd normally have to travel to Las Vegas or Los Angeles. But instead, visit Issaquah, a mere 30-minute drive from Seattle. Here, at the Illusionz Magical Entertainment Center, master magician Steffan Soule's *Mysterian* production offers audiences a mind-blowing show full of "dramagic" experience with participation from those in attendance.

Illusionz is the Northwest's first major venue for world-class magic. It offers numerous opportunities to watch or create magic and illusion, and to see magic masters as they work their age-old art. The *Mysterian* show is staged in a state-of-the-art theater. But Illusionz also has a smaller sleight-of-hand stage for an up-close view of basic magic tricks. The facility is peppered with interactive illusions (such as the black light entryways).

For those who prefer magic in the form of games, the Illusionz arcade runs the gamut. It includes rows of video games, an 18-hole putt-putt golf course, an automated rock climbing wall, laser tag and Magicastle, an inflatable building for preschoolers.

There's even a Magic store on-site, a perfect place to pick up a trick deck of cards or a magic top hat.

SEASONS AND TIMES
➤ *Mysterian* production: Fri, 8 pm; Sat, 3 pm and 8 pm; Sun, 3 pm. Close-up Magic Theatre: Fri, 9:30 pm; Sat, 5:15 pm and 9:30 pm. Arcade: Mon—Thu, 10 am—10 pm; Fri—Sat, 10 am—midnight; Sun, noon—8 pm.

COST
➤ *Mysterian* production: Adults $15, children (under 13) $10. Close-up Magic Theatre: Individuals $5. Arcade: Passes range from $10.95 to $25.95 per person.

GETTING THERE
➤ By car, from Seattle Center, head east on Mercer St. to I-5 South. Take I-5 S. to the 1-90 E. Exit and head east on I-90 toward Issaquah. Take Exit 15 and travel south on Issaquah/Renton Rd. At the first set of lights, turn east onto N.W. Gilman Blvd. Go through one stoplight at 12th Ave. N.W. Then turn south into Town & Country Square. About 35 minutes from Seattle Center.

NEARBY
➤ Downtown Issaquah, Village Theatre, Cougar Mountain Zoo, Lake Sammamish, Cougar Mountain hiking trails.

COMMENT
➤ Plan a 2- to 3-hour visit.

Lights and Lasers
IMAX™ AND LASER DOME

**Pacific Science Center
200 – 2nd Ave. N., Seattle
(206) 443-4629 (IMAX™ Theatre),
(206) 443-2850 (Laser Dome)
www.pacsci.org and
www.laserfantasy.com/Laser_Shows/seattle.html**

The Pacific Science Center (PSC) is home to two giant-screen theaters that play movies filmed at the largest frame size available—ten times larger than 35 mm film. The Eames IMAX™ theater is PSC's first and has a three-and-a-half-story high, 60-foot wide screen. The Boeing IMAX™ theater opened in 1998 and features an unbelievable six-story high, 80-foot wide screen. Shows are presented on a wide range of topics, from wolves to documentaries on Antarctica. But to really get into the action, plan to see a 3-D show at the Boeing theater. When audience members put on 3-D glasses, the screen comes alive. Kids often try to "grab" at objects projected in front of them.

Looking for something that's tamer? Then head to the Adobe Laser Dome. It's literally a "laid back" show. There are seats, but many audience members prefer to lie on their backs and stare up at the "sky," where choreographed laser lights and shapes are projected while music plays in the background. Show themes change throughout the year. Popular family matinees have included *Peter and the Wolf*, holiday specials such as the *Nutcracker Fantasy* and *Holiday Magic*, and the teen pop favorite, *POP ROX*.

SEASONS AND TIMES

➤ IMAX™: Year-round, Mon–Fri, 11 am–6 pm; Sat–Sun, 11 am–9 pm. Call for exact times. Laser shows: Year-round, daily. Call for exact times. Both closed Thanksgiving and Christmas.

COST

➤ IMAX™: Ranges from $5.75 to $10 per person. Laser shows (when purchased with PSC admission): Matinees $4.50, evenings Fri–Sun $7.50; Wed–Thu $5. Combination admission prices available for Pacific Science Center exhibits and IMAX™ movies and Laser Shows.

GETTING THERE

➤ By car, from I-5 take the Mercer St. Exit and head west towards the Space Needle. Some free parking is available on nearby streets. During special events, parking fees at Center parking lots are based on number of people in vehicle (discounts for 2 or more). Expect to pay between $6 and $12 for all-day parking.

➤ By public transit, more than a dozen Metro bus routes service Seattle Center. Call Metro Transit for route and schedule information (206) 553-3000. Or, catch a ride on the monorail from downtown.

NEARBY

➤ Seattle Center, downtown Seattle, Pike Place Market, Waterfront.

COMMENT

➤ IMAX™ movies run about 45 minutes. Laser shows run about 40 minutes. Evening laser shows are geared to teens and adults. Late seating not allowed, so plan to arrive at least 20 minutes before show time.

SIMILAR ATTRACTION

➤ **Seattle IMAX™ Dome** · 180-degree dome screen with 6-channel surround sound. Pier 59, 1483 Alaskan Way (206) 662-1869. www.seattleimaxdome.com

An Age-old Art
NORTHWEST PUPPET
CENTER & MUSEUM

9123 - 15th Ave. N.E., Seattle
(206) 523-2579
www.nwpuppet.org

P uppeteers from around the world mark Seattle on their places-to-go map. You should too. Each year the Northwest Puppet Center stages seven family-oriented productions, including several played by visiting puppetry companies. The diverse line-up of programs offers families prime entertainment and multicultural education at the same time. You might see a production from an Indian or Japanese company, or a show where all the puppets perform underwater.

The artisans from the Carter Family Marionettes, the center's resident puppet company, have traveled the globe to learn age-old puppetry arts from the masters. The center also offers various puppetry and puppet-making workshops and a wonderful basement museum of puppetry. Along with character puppets from favorite productions, the museum includes several antiques and a kids play area.

SEASONS AND TIMES
➤ Year-round: Fri, 7:30 am; Sat—Sun, 1 pm and 3 pm. Call for group information and reservations.

COST
➤ Adults $8.50, seniors (65 and over) $7, children $6.50.

GETTING THERE
➤ By car, from Seattle Center, head east on Mercer St. to I-5 North. Take I-5 N. to the Lake City Way Exit. Turn north on 15th Ave. N.E. and continue to 92nd St. The center is on the corner of 92nd and 15th. About 15 minutes from Seattle Center.

➤ By public transit, board Metro bus 73, 77 or 78 and ride it to 15th. Call Metro Transit for route and schedule information (206) 553-3000.

NEARBY
➤ Green Lake.

COMMENTS
➤ Plan a 1- to 2-hour visit to see a show and the museum.

A *Moving Experience*
PACIFIC NORTHWEST BALLET

301 Mercer St., Seattle
(206) 441-9411, (206) 441-2424 (tickets)
www.pnb.org

For many families in Seattle, a trip to Pacific Northwest Ballet's (PNB) annual production of *The Nutcracker* is a much-anticipated holiday tradition. With magical sets designed by Maurice Sendak and larger-than-life choreography, this classic ballet has kids written all over it— especially when seen as part of PNB's holiday brunch event in mid-November.

Although *The Nutcracker* attracts the most families, PNB offers wonderfully accessible dances appropriate for young viewers throughout the season. Each year, company directors try to include favorite tales for children such as *Sleeping Beauty, A Midsummer-Night's Dream, Cinderella* and *Swan Lake.* PNB's more challenging productions are suitable for older kids and teens who will delight in the art and physicality of classical dance.

For a fun and educational extra, drop in 45 minutes before any regular season performance and check out the free ballet previews. These behind-the-scenes discussions are a great way for young people to gain a better understanding of what they are going to see. PNB also has a dance school that offers classes for children starting at age five. The school's non-audition drop-in Summer Open Program is available to all, no experience necessary.

SEASONS AND TIMES
➤ Sept—June: Evening shows, 7:30 pm; Matinees, 2 pm. Call for schedule of events.

COST
➤ Varies. From $15 to $110 per person. Half-price tickets for students and seniors available 1 hour prior to curtain time depending on availability (*Nutcracker* excluded). Group rates available for 10 or more.

GETTING THERE
➤ By car, from I-5 take the Mercer St. Exit and head west to the Space Needle. Located on north side of Seattle Center. Park on street or in the Seattle Center parking garage located between 3rd and 4th Ave. N. on Mercer St.
➤ By public transit, Metro bus service routes include 1, 2, 3, 4, 8, 13, 15, 16, 18, 19, 24, 33, 45, 81 and 82. Call Metro Transit for route and schedule information (206) 553-3000.

NEARBY
➤ Downtown Seattle, Seattle Center, International Fountain, Space Needle, Experience Music Project, Waterfront, Monorail, Pacific Science Center.

COMMENT
➤ Plan a 2- to 4-hour visit depending on the length of the show. PNB store in lobby.

SIMILAR ATTRACTIONS
➤ **Olympic Ballet Theatre** · Tickets from $12 to $25. Dance school (425) 774-7570. www.olyballet.com
➤ **Kaleidoscope Dance Company** · Tickets usually under $5. School performances. Company comprised of children 8 to 14. (206) 363-7281. www.creativedance.org

The Play's the Thing
SEATTLE CHILDREN'S
THEATRE

**201 Thomas St., Seattle
(206) 443-0807, (206) 441-3322 (tickets)
www.sct.org**

As the second largest professional theater for children in the nation, the Seattle Children's Theatre (SCT) boasts top-notch productions and innovative programming for families. For more than 26 years, the SCT has been thrilling kids and grown-ups alike with creative stage productions in drama, comedy and musical theater.

Visiting SCT lets you see magic and life breathed into classics such as *The Velveteen Rabbit*, *Stellaluna* and *The Red Balloon*. SCT also hosts many world premiere productions and puts on new plays in its two state-of-the-art theaters.

Each season SCT presents shows that appeal to an array of ages, from toddlers to teens. The company's professional actors are educators as well as artists. Shows are followed by a question and answer session, where audience members are invited to learn more about the production, characters and staging of a show.

If your kids can't get enough, sign them up for SCT's Drama School. Youngsters aged 3 to 19 can participate in a variety of classes and workshops. Call (206) 443-0807 for details and a schedule. The school also offers one of the country's premier acting programs for deaf students. Led by co-founder and current Program Director Billy Seago, the Deaf Youth Drama Program serves 3,300 students annually. This project facilitates an integration of deaf, hard-of-hearing and hearing students through in-school residencies, the creation and presentation of the Deaf Kids Drama Festivals, theater workshops and summer stage productions.

SEASONS AND TIMES
➤ Sept—June: Fri, 7 pm; Sat—Sun, 2 pm and 5:30 pm. Call for a season schedule.

COST
➤ Matinees: Adults $22, seniors (65 and up), full-time students and children (1 and up) $15.50. Evening Shows: $1 less. Season tickets available.

GETTING THERE
➤ By car, from I-5, take the Mercer St. Exit and head west to the Space Needle. Located in Seattle Center. Park on street or at parking garages or nearby lots.
➤ By public transit, Metro bus service routes include 1, 2, 3, 4, 8, 13, 15, 16, 18, 19, 24, 33, 45, 81 and 82. Call Metro Transit for route and schedule information (206) 553-3000.

NEARBY
➤ Downtown Seattle, Seattle Center, International Fountain, Space Needle, Experience Music Project, Waterfront, Monorail, Pacific Science Center.

COMMENT
➤ To avoid refreshment lines, purchase snacks before the show. Diaper changing station and in-theater crying rooms available for restless children. Great gift shop on-site. Plan a 1- to 2-hour visit.

The Music Makers
SEATTLE SYMPHONY

Benaroya Hall, 200 University St., Seattle
(206) 215-4700, (206) 215-4747 (tickets)
www.seattlesymphony.org

The Seattle Symphony offers Seattle residents and visitors a plethora of family-oriented classical music programs. One of the most popular is the Tiny Tots program for children under five and their families. It features a variety of dynamic performers working with symphony musicians to introduce youngsters to the world of music through games, stories and songs.

Are your kids a little older? Then send them to Symphony's Discover Music shows designed for children aged 5 to 12. These shows vary from storytelling concerts to *Introducing the Composer* programs. Pre-concert activities allow children to learn about music and participate in hands-on exercises aimed at enhancing the day's performance. With billings such as *Beethoven Lives Upstairs*, *How Gimquat Found Her Song* and *Tales of Truth and Make Believe*, your kids will get hooked on classical music faster than you can say orchestra.

The Seattle Symphony offers educational programs too, from free concerts played by student musicians to pre-concert lectures. While music is the main attraction at Benaroya Hall, the hall itself is worth a visit. Opened to the applause of architects and sound experts worldwide in 1998, Benaroya is acoustics construction at its very best.

SEASONS AND TIMES
➤ Sept—July: Varies depending on program. Call for schedule and times.

COST
➤ Varies depending on program. Call for details. Tiny Tots and Discover Music programs: Range from $9.50 to $14.

GETTING THERE
➤ By car, from Seattle Center, travel south on 3rd Ave. Benaroya is located on 3rd between Union and University streets.
➤ By public transit, take any Metro bus headed southbound on 3rd. Call Metro Transit for route and schedule information (206) 553-3000.

NEARBY
➤ Downtown Seattle, Seattle Center, Waterfront, Monorail, Pike Place Market, Pioneer Square.

COMMENTS
➤ Symphonica Store and snack bar within building. Plan a 2- to 4-hour visit, depending on show.

All the World's a Stage
STUDIO EAST

**402 - 6th St. S., Kirkland
(425) 827-3123
www.studio-east.org**

At Studio East, students in the performing arts training program share their talents on the theater's stage in such classic productions as *Sound of Music* and *Cinderella*. Students audition and rehearse intensively, then perform four of these Mainstage productions a year, each for a three-week run.

Studio East's offshoot, StoryBook Theatre, features adult actors in shows geared for tykes aged 3 to 9. Performing in four venues in the Seattle area, StoryBook Theatre puts on plays based on traditional fairy tales rewritten to appeal to the humor and attention span of today's youth. There is lots of audience participation, plenty of jokes and gentle lessons. Many of the stories have been updated to include more contemporary endings. *Cinderella*, for instance, ends with Cinderella and the Prince going out for Chinese food. In *The Three Little Pigs*, the wolf works for "homeporker.com," while the vegetarian wolf in *Little Red Riding Hood* is in search of something healthy to eat (not Grandma).

StoryBook Theatre productions are popular with school groups, who can attend at reduced prices. Performances are held at Kirkland Performance Center (350 Kirkland Ave., Kirkland), PUD Auditorium (2320 California St., Everett), Broadway Performance Hall (Seattle Central Community College, 1625 Broadway St., Seattle) and Carco Theater (1717 Maple Valley Hwy., Renton).

SEASONS AND TIMES
➤ Storybook Theatre: Oct–May, Sat–Sun. Weekday performances available for schools. Call for schedule, times and details. Student performances: Dec–May. Dates and times vary depending on show. Call for details.

COST
➤ StoryBook Theatre: General admission $7, school groups $5. Student performances: Adults $8 to $15, seniors and students $6 to $10.

GETTING THERE
➤ To get to Studio East from Seattle Center, head east on Mercer St. to I-5 North. Take I-5 N. and exit at the SR-520 Exit. Continue on SR-520 east to the Lake Washington Blvd. Exit to Kirkland. Go north on Lake Washington Blvd. At the "Y" at Carillon Pt., turn northeast on to Lakeview Dr. (which becomes N.E. 68th St.) Continue to 6th St. S. then turn west. About 25 minutes from Seattle Center. For directions to other venues, call Studio East or visit their website.

COMMENT
➤ StoryBook Theatre shows are 55 minutes long. Length of student shows vary.

Puppet Performances at
THISTLE THEATRE

(206) 524-3388
www.thistletheatre.org

This unique puppet troupe presents six puppet productions each season, using a Japanese form of puppetry called bunraku. The puppeteers are dressed in black and are visible on stage as they operate the puppets by rods. Past shows have included *Aesop's Fables*, *Scheherazade* (accompanied by a philharmonic orchestra), *The Tales of Beatrix Potter* and a bilingual show, *Muchas Chickens*. A holiday favorite is *Merry Chris Mouse*. Shows have live music and feature original compositions by Sue Ennis, a member of the Lovemongers.

Thistle Theatre performs its shows at three locations in the Seattle area: Burien Little Theater (425 S.W. 144th, Burien), Moore Theater at Sacred Heart School (9442 N.E. 14th, Bellevue) and Langston Hughes Cultural Center (104 17th Ave. S., Seattle). Discounts available on shows for school groups held in Burien. Thistle Theatre also performs at school assemblies and is available to entertain at birthday parties and other special events. Shows are appropriate for preschool children and older.

SEASONS AND TIMES
‣ Sept–Apr. Show times vary by show and location. Most performances are on weekend afternoons. Call for details.

COST
‣ Adults $8, seniors and children (under 18) $6. Season tickets available.

COMMENT
‣ Shows last an hour.

Seeing Future Stars at
YOUTH THEATRE
NORTHWEST

8805 S.E. 40th St., Mercer Island
(206) 232-4145, (206) 232-2202 (box office)
www.youththeatre.org

For some youthful entertainment, head to Youth Theatre Northwest (YTN). This theater boasts six productions each year featuring student performers, directors and set designers. Some recent shows have included *Beauty and the Beast*, *Alice's Adventures in Wonderland*, *Jack and the Beanstalk* and *Guys and Dolls*. Young audience members especially enjoy the question-and-answer sessions after each performance. They can learn how particular stage tricks were done, find out how long it takes student actors to memorize their lines and discover how much work goes into creating a play.

YTN offers classes for ages 3 to 18, camps and partnership programs with schools. "Dramatic" birthday parties are available too—they include an art project and drama workshop that goes along with the theme of the current main stage play, or follow a customized theme.

SEASONS AND TIMES
→ Aug—May: Fri, 7:30 pm; Sat, 2 and 7:30 pm; Sun, 2 pm.

COST
→ $9 per person. Season tickets available.

GETTING THERE
→ By car, from Seattle Center, head east on Mercer St. to I-5 South. Take I-5 S. to the I-90 E. Exit. Proceed on I-90 to the Island Crest Way Exit. Travel south on Island Crest Way to S.E. 40th St. Proceed east to the theater. About 20 minutes from Seattle Center.
→ By public transit, board Sound Transit 550 Express bus at the Westlake bus tunnel downtown. Get off at the Mercer Island Park & Ride and board Metro bus 204 to south Mercer Island. Get off at 86th St. and S.E. 40th St. and walk 2 blocks east to the theater. Call Metro Transit for route and schedule information (206) 553-3000.

Other Family Theater Options

The Seattle area and nearby towns are home to a vibrant theater scene, including Broadway musicals on tour, productions by local theater groups and community performances geared to children. Here are some additional venues and production companies with shows appropriate for families.

Bainbridge Performing Arts Center
200 Madison Ave. N., Bainbridge Island
(206) 842-8569

The center offers an array of family-oriented productions and educational opportunities. Costs vary. About 1 hour from Seattle, including 20-minute ferry ride.

Pied Piper Presents
Everett Performing Arts Center
2710 Wetmore Ave., Everett
(425) 257-6363, (425) 257-8600 (tickets)
www.piedpiperpresents.org

Pied Piper offers wonderful theater for families. Tickets $8 to $15. Discounts and packages available.

Seattle Shakespeare Company/Festival

Performance Studio in Seattle Center, Seattle
(206) 733-8222
http://frak.snowtop.com

Oct–Apr: Thu–Sun: Family show, Sun at 2 pm. Tickets range from $10 to $22. Season tickets available.

Taproot Theatre

204 N. 85th St., Seattle
(206) 781-9707
www.taproottheatre.org

Christian-themed musicals and dramas, including annual Christmas show. Wed–Sat, evenings; Sat, matinees. $14 to $24.

The 5th Avenue Theatre (page 185)

1308 5th Ave., Seattle
(206) 292-ARTS
www.fifthavenuetheatre.org

This historic theater presents a season of Broadway musicals. Most productions are suitable for ages 8 and up. Tickets range from $18 to $70.

The Paramount Theatre

911 Pine St., Seattle
(206) 292-ARTS (2787)
www.theparamount.com

Seattle Theater Group offers Broadway and off-Broadway productions as well as dance, musicals and silent film at the historic Paramount Theatre and Moore Theatre. Tickets range from $10 to $50.

Village Theatre
303 Front St., Issaquah (425) 392-2202
2710 Wetmore Ave., Everett (425) 257-8600
www.villagetheatre.org

Original and classic musicals are presented on two stages in Issaquah, and at the Everett Performing Arts Center in Everett. The KIDSTAGE program offers theater classes for children with two annual productions.

Community Centers and Libraries
www.kcls.org (King County Library System),
www.spl.org (Seattle Public Library)

Free entertainment for children can often be found right in your own neighborhood at local libraries, community centers or parks. Summer and holiday programs at libraries feature storytellers, sing-alongs, multicultural music and dance, dramatic performances, magic shows and more. This is a great way to introduce very young children to the joys of watching live shows. Parks and Recreation Departments offer concert and performance series at parks in the summer and community centers the rest of the year.

CHAPTER 7

ANIMALS, FARMS & ZOOS

Introduction

Kids love petting and feeding farm animals. It's easy to do at three public parks in the area: Forest Park in Everett, Kelsey Creek Community Park and Farm in Bellevue and Farrel-McWhirter Park in Redmond. Each has an animal farm with special events and classes for kids.

To view animals and marine life from around the world and learn about conservation, visit the highly acclaimed Woodland Park Zoo, Seattle Aquarium, Cougar Mountain Zoo and Point Defiance Zoo and Aquarium.

If it's farm food and fun you're after, you'll find them at Remlinger Farms in Redmond—the local leader in "agritainment." Their traditional U-pick berries and pumpkin patches are supplemented with family-oriented activities, including a steam train, pony rides, an animal barn, a farm theater and special seasonal festivals. Other farms in the area feature U-pick produce, as well as October harvest events and Christmas trees.

At the end of this chapter, you'll find a list of places where you can take the kids to see animals and nature for free. Included are wetland parks on Lake Washington, a salmon hatchery in Issaquah and quaint Country Village in Bothell.

The Cat's Meow
COUGAR MOUNTAIN ZOOLOGICAL PARK

5410 – 194th Ave. S.E., Issaquah
(425) 391-5508
www.cougarmountainzoo.org

Colorful, talkative macaws, wide-eyed lemurs and Formosan elk may not immediately come to mind when visiting Seattle, but that is exactly what you will find at Cougar Mountain Zoological Park in Issaquah.

The park is known worldwide for its endangered wildlife conservation efforts. It is divided into ten Worlds: Mountain Lions, Reindeer, Large Macaws, Antelopes, Cheetahs, Formosan Elk, Lemurs, Cranes, and two other exhibits that rotate through the zoo annually. Each section features up-close-and-personal views of animals in indoor and outdoor settings. They have been landscaped to provide the most natural habitat possible. Feeding facilities enable you to view the animals at mealtime.

Don't be surprised if you are cornered by the resident alpaca in search of apple wedges ($1 a feeding). It is all part of the zoo's interactive design. Kids love the "permanent residents"—a herd of bronze animal statues that are perfect for climbing. Cougar Mountain's informative park volunteers are eager to share their knowledge about exotic and endangered wildlife. Ask a volunteer to feed the lemurs a grape and watch the flying and leaping begin!

The zoo offers numerous classes and educational programs; most highlight the issues faced by endangered species. The public is invited to participate in the zoo's conservation efforts and take part in internships. Pre-scheduled programs include guided tours, lectures, special events and celebrations, birthday parties and school outreach programs.

SEASONS AND TIMES
➤ Mar—Oct: Fri—Sun, 10 am—5 pm. Pre-scheduled programs offered year-round.

COST
➤ Adults $8, seniors (over 61) $6.50, youths (4 to 15) $5.50, tots (2 to 3) $4, under 2 free. Group discounts and memberships available. AAA Members with card receive discount of $0.50.

GETTING THERE
➤ By car, from Seattle Center, head east on Mercer St. to I-5 South. Take I-5 S. to the I-90 Exit heading east across Lake Washington. Follow I-90 E. to Exit 15. Head south onto 17th Ave. N.W. Turn west on Newport Way, and then turn south on S.E. 54th St. at the Zoo Landmark Sign. The Cougar Mountain Zoo is located approximately 1/2 mile up S.E. 54th St. Free parking on site. About 30 minutes from Seattle Center.

NEARBY
➤ Historic Issaquah, Lake Sammamish State Park, Bellevue's Kelsey Creek Farm.

COMMENT
➤ Strollers with all-terrain wheels are recommended. Plan a 1-to 2-hour visit. Longer if you participate in classes, tours or special events.

Fun on the Farm
FARREL-McWHIRTER PARK

19545 Redmond Rd., Redmond
(425) 556-2300

Many families in the King County city of Redmond have visited this park, however it is less well known in Seattle. You will want to check out this eastside "secret," especially if your youngsters enjoy seeing farm animals and learning about farm life.

The 70-acre property was generously willed to the city of Redmond by its owner, Elise Farrel-McWhirter. It became a public park in the mid-1970s. As a working farm, the city has developed it into a wonderful learning facility. Children can ride ponies, feed farm animals at Breakfast With the Animals programs, work in the garden and explore the farm at parent-child classes. A preschool meets here several days a week as well.

Seasonal events, craft classes, camps and other recreational programs are offered year-round. You don't have to register for special programs to meet the animals. Drop by anytime to visit the rabbits, chickens, pigs, goats, ponies and "Ivory" the albino cow. Take a walk on the paved Charlotte's Trail and on the other trails along the creek. Bring a picnic and let your kids loose at the playground. Don't miss the unique restroom—it's a converted silo.

SEASONS AND TIMES

➤ Park: Year-round, daily, 8 am—dusk. Farm: Year-round, daily, 9 am—5 pm.

COST

➤ Free. Fees for classes, camps and special events.

GETTING THERE

➤ By car, from Seattle Center, head east on Mercer St. to I-5 North. Take I-5 N. to SR-520 and proceed east on SR-520 until it ends and turns into Avondale Rd. Take Avondale for 1 mile and turn south on Novelty Hill Rd. Go 1/2 mile and turn on to Redmond Rd. Free parking on site. About 30 minutes from Seattle Center.

NEARBY

➤ Marymoor Park, Redmond Town Center.

COMMENT

➤ Plan a 1- to 2-hour visit.

Get Down and Dirty at
FOREST PARK

802 Mukilteo Blvd., Everett
(425) 257-8300
www.ci.everett.wa.us/everett/parks

If getting a little muddy is no problem, Forest Park Animal Farm is a must-see for families. It is one of the region's best animal barns because it is rarely crowded and always hopping. The park's petting zoo allows you to roam in the open animal pens to feed pigs, goats and chickens. Don't be surprised if one of the goats plunks his mucky hooves on your chest to beg a pellet or two. Wear clothing that you don't mind getting dirty. The horse corrals are not open to visitors, but pony rides are offered for free throughout the summer.

The Animal Farm is not the only reason for visiting Forest Park. The park's huge playgrounds (one for toddlers, one for older kids) provide hours of climbing, swinging, swaying and bouncing fun. The Swim Center (425-257-8309) has a spacious, heated pool and offers programs to families and kids and special events at very low cost. The large lawn is great for birthday parties, volleyball, badminton or touch football. Hiking paths, horseshoes, tennis courts, an open picnic area, numerous park buildings and halls round out the accouterments.

SEASONS AND TIMES
➤ Park: Year-round, daily, dawn—dusk. Animal barn: Apr—Sept, daily, 9 am—5 pm.

COST
➤ Park, animal barn and playground: Free. Swim Center: Adults $2, under 17 $1.50. Family nights ($4.50 per family) are offered throughout the year. Call for a schedule. Fees may apply for special events and classes.

GETTING THERE
➤ By car, from Seattle Center, head east on Mercer St. to I-5 North. Take I-5 N. to Exit 192/Broadway. Stay in right lane and take the second exit ramp onto 41st St. Head west on 41st through 2 traffic lights. The road turns up a hillside and becomes Mukilteo Blvd. The park is at the top of the curve. Free parking on site. About 45 minutes from Seattle Center.

➤ By public transit, take Sound Transit bus 512 from downtown
Seattle at 4th and Union to Everett. Transfer to Everett Transit 23
South to Forest Park. Call Community Transit for route and schedule
information (800) 562-1375.

NEARBY
➤ Children's Museum of Snohomish County, Jetty Island, Everett
Performing Arts Center, Boeing Everett Factory Tour.

COMMENT
➤ Plan at least a half-day visit.

A *Taste of Country Living* at
KELSEY CREEK
COMMUNITY PARK
& FARM

13204 S.E. 8th Pl., Bellevue
(425) 452-7688
www.ci.bellevue.wa.us/parks/majorparks/kelsey.htm

L ooking for first-hand farm experience,
without having to travel far? Pack up the van
and drive to Bellevue's Kelsey Creek, a 150-
acre park that's home to a working farm.

Kids love visiting the barns to meet ponies,
chickens, rabbits, cows and other animals. They are
behind fences or in cages, however you can pat a
goat's nose through the fence or stand on the railing
to peer down at a family of pigs. Kelsey Creek offers
wonderful educational opportunities for families and

schools, including farm experience tours and hands-on classes in animal care. There are plenty of holiday events, such as the annual pumpkin patch and farm fair in October.

Have time left over? Take a walk on one of the park's numerous hiking trails. Kelsey Creek's boundaries include a lush forested area and wetland habitat. For families with small children, the mile-long gravel trail that surrounds the back pasture is toddler-friendly and stroller accessible. Head to the park's playground with its wooden house, seesaw and slides. Nearby Kelsey Creek is a great place to watch waterfowl.

If you have history buffs in the family, stop at the Frazier cabin. It was built in 1888 and is one of Bellevue's oldest structures. It looks like any old cabin you might encounter in a wooded forest, but holds the distinction of being the first in Bellevue.

SEASONS AND TIMES
➤ Year-round: Daily, dawn—dusk. Animal viewing hours are weather dependent, but generally 8 am—4 pm.

COST
➤ Park and Farm: Free. Fees may apply to some classes and special programs.

GETTING THERE
➤ By car, from Seattle Center, head east on Mercer St. to I-5 North. Take I-5 N. to the SR 520 Exit and head east. Take the I-405 S. Exit off of SR 520. Follow I-405 to the S.E. 8th St. and head east off the exit. The road will wind through a residential area. Go through the first stop sign. When the street comes to a "T" (at the second stop sign), turn south onto S.E. 8th Place. The park will be on the west side. Park

for free along the road or in the parking lot at the north end of park. About 30 minutes from Seattle Center.

➤ By public transit, take Metro bus 550 from the Seattle bus tunnel (downtown at Westlake Center) and ride it to Bellevue bus transit station. Transfer to bus 271 (Lake Hills Exchange) and ask the driver to stop at Kelsey Creek. Call Metro Transit for route and schedule information (206) 553-3000.

NEARBY
➤ Bellevue Square, Bellevue Art Museum, Mercer Slough Nature Park, Bellevue Botanical Gardens, Rosalie Whyel Museum of Doll Art.

COMMENT
➤ Plan a 1- to 2-hour visit.

Animals A to Z
POINT DEFIANCE ZOO
& AQUARIUM

5400 N. Pearl St., Tacoma
(253) 591-5337
www.pdza.org

Though it is smaller than Seattle's Woodland Park Zoo (page 158), the Point Defiance Zoo and Aquarium has plenty of first-rate exhibits to see in its 29 acres. In fact, the zoo's smaller size is an advantage for children. Walks between the displays are not overwhelming and animals are easy to find in their naturalistic habitats.

One of the zoo's nine-themed areas is the Arctic Tundra habitat. It's home to an award-winning polar bear exhibit with two playful young cubs. Catch sight of sea otters, seals, sea lions, beluga whales and puffins of the Arctic in the Rocky Shores exhibit. Stop in at the Elephant House where three Asian elephants share their space with two endangered leopards. More than 50 sharks swim in the Sharks—The Survivors exhibit, where interactive displays educate visitors and dispel myths about these animals.

The Discovery Reef Aquarium features a tropical environment with warm temperatures, birds and colorful fish while the North Pacific Aquarium highlights species native to the Northwest. At the World of Adaptations, you will find a diverse collection of animals—from birds, insects and frogs to naked mole rats, bats and more. The endangered red wolf makes its home in this area too—the zoo is the official survival and breeding center for the species. Rounding out the exhibits are Penguin Point and Animal Farm, where visitors can get close to goats, reindeer, llamas and pygmies.

Seasonal events make the zoo popular year-round. Overnight camp-outs called ZooSnoozes are held in the spring and summer. In December, the annual Zoolights festival lights up the zoo at night during the holiday season with thousands of light displays (animal exhibits aren't open during Zoolights).

SEASONS AND TIMES

➤ Summer (Memorial Day–Labor Day): Daily, 10 am–7 pm. Closed third Friday in July. Winter (Labor Day–Memorial Day): Daily, 10 am–4 pm or 6 pm, depending. Closed Thanksgiving and Christmas.

COST

➤ Adults $7.25, seniors (over 61) and youths (4 to 13) $5.50, under 4 free. Discounts for Tacoma residents.

GETTING THERE

➤ By car, from Seattle Center, head east on Mercer St. to I-5 South. Follow 1-5 S. to Exit 132. Go west and follow the signs to Hwy. 16 W. (Bremerton/Gig Harbor). Take the 6th Ave. Exit and turn west. Turn north onto Pearl St., which dead-ends at Point Defiance Park. Follow the signs to the zoo parking lots. About 45 minutes from Seattle.

NEARBY

➤ Point Defiance Park, Vashon Ferry, Washington State History Museum.

COMMENT

➤ Plan a 2-hour visit. Longer if you take in some of the other attractions at Point Defiance Park (page 89).

Tons of Fun at
REMLINGER FARMS

32610 N.E. 32nd St., Carnation
(425) 451-8740
www.remlingerfarms.com

Western Washington is home to a number of family-friendly working farms where children can meet animals and have fun learning about farming. Remlinger Farms is one of the best. It offers kid-oriented petting yards, activities, festivals and events from May to October. The farm provides charm to please parents and more than enough amusement for kids.

Depending on weather and season, your admission to the Family Fun Fair covers farm pony trail rides, the Tolt River Railroad mini-steam train ride, the 4-H Animal Barnyard, the Mine-Twister roller coaster, the Northwest Canoe Adventure, a hay maze and hay jump, the playground and a swing carousel. If that's not enough, your ticket also includes admission to the Farm Theatre with live entertainment. It's easy to forget that you are on a working farm with so many exciting things to do, but remember to tour the actual farm, too!

If Halloween is a big holiday in your family, be sure to stop by in October so your kids can ogle the fields of ripe pumpkins. Anytime of the year, stop at the Remlinger Restaurant and Bakery (425-333-4135). The farm is famous for its pies and with good reason. A great kid's menu ensures the little ones are happy.

SEASONS AND TIMES
➤ Working Farm: Early May—late Oct, daily, 11 am—5 pm. Theme park: Early May—late Oct, daily, 10 am—6 pm.

COST
➤ Mon—Fri, $5 per person; Sat—Sun, adults $8, seniors $7, children $9 (unlimited use of rides and park).

GETTING THERE
➤ By car, from Seattle Center, head east on Mercer St. to I-5 North. Take I-5 N. and exit at SR-520. Head east on SR-520 to the Redmond/Fall City Exit. Access Hwy. 202 (Redmond-Fall City Rd.)

and head east for about 9 miles toward Fall City. Look for a blue "tourist activity" sign and turn north onto Tolt Hill Rd. Follow Tolt Hill to Remlinger Farms. Free parking on site. About 45 minutes from Seattle Center.

NEARBY
➤ Nestle-Carnation Dairy Farm, Snoqualmie Falls, North Bend, Snoqualmie Railroad, historic Issaquah.

COMMENT
➤ Plan a 2- to 3-hour visit.

Underwater Magic at the
SEATTLE AQUARIUM

**Pier 59 on the Waterfront, Seattle
(206) 386-4320 (Aquarium) or (206) 622-1868
(IMAX™ Dome)
www.seattleaquarium.org**

Can you imagine coming nose to nose with a reef shark or communicating with a sea otter? It's easy at the Seattle Aquarium. Visitors can get close to some of the Pacific Coast's most captivating marine animals. Your encounter begins as soon as you enter the Aquarium's foyer, where tank after tank of sea life helps you make the transition from shore to ocean.

After gazing at the tanks, head to the Aquarium's 400,000-gallon Underwater Dome. Here you'll find an eye-boggling panoramic view of sea life in Puget Sound, complete with over 1,000 fish. The Dome will quiet even the most fidgety kid. Call the Aquarium to inquire about feeding times. The divers who enter the tank to feed the fish are as mesmerizing as the fish themselves.

The Aquarium's outdoor exhibits are equally enticing—and better still, they are hands-on. Kids can reach down and touch starfish, urchins and mussels. The Aquarium is among an elite group of marine educational facilities and holds the title "Coastal America Ecosystem Learning Center." The designation means the Aquarium receives special financial, exhibit and expert support from 14 other marine organizations committed to protecting and restoring coastal environments.

The facility also offers a long list of special events and kid features throughout the year. Some of the most popular include the Salmon Homecoming (with numerous activities for children) in September and the Sea Sounds summer concert series. The IMAX™ Dome Theater is located at the Aquarium, so pack some snacks and make your visit a full-day adventure.

SEASONS AND TIMES
➤ Aquarium: Summer (Memorial Day—Labor Day), daily, 10 am—7 pm. Winter (Labor Day—Memorial Day): Daily, 10 am—5 pm. IMAX™ Dome: Varies.

COST
➤ Aquarium: Adults $8.50, seniors and disabled patrons $7.50, youths (6 to 18) $5.75, children (3 to 5) $3.75, under 3 free. Discounts for residents of King County. IMAX™ Dome: Adults $7, seniors (over 64) $6.50, youths (6 to 18) $6, under 6 free. $2 for second film on same day.

GETTING THERE
➤ By car, from the east side of Seattle Center, take Broad St. west towards Puget Sound. Turn south on Alaskan Way and continue to metered parking near viaduct or park in nearby lots. About 10 minutes from Seattle Center.
➤ By public transit, walk from Seattle Center to the waterfront via Broad St. Take the Waterfront Street Car Route 99 to the Aquarium midway along the waterfront. Call Metro Transit for route and schedule information (206) 553-3000.

NEARBY
➤ Waterfront, Pike Street Hill Climb, Pike Place Market, Pioneer Square, Safeco Field.

COMMENT
➤ Plan a 1-to 2-hour visit.

Rural Adventures
U-PICK FARMS

L ess than an hour from the big city, families can pick their own produce during spring and summer, select pumpkins in autumn and find the perfect Christmas tree in winter. Besides these fresh-grown delights, most farms offer special seasonal events and activities to entice city folks to the countryside. October is an especially busy month at many farms, with pumpkin patches, harvest festivals, corn and hay mazes and more. For a complete guide to local farms in King, Pierce, Skagit and Snohomish counties, pick up a free copy of *Farm Fresh Guide* at local libraries, or visit their website http://dnr.metrokc.gov/wlr/farms/FGfarmguide.htm. Here are a few local favorites:

Biringer Farm
Hwy. 529, Marysville
(425) 259-0255
www.biringerfarm.com

Open mid-June—July for berries; Aug—Oct for corn maze and pumpkins; Nov—Dec for Christmas trees. Seasonal festivals with tours, rides and other activities.

Bolles Organic Farm
17930 Tualco Loop Rd., Monroe
(360) 805-1980

Organic produce available in season.

Craven Farm & Pumpkin Patch
13817 Short School Rd., Snohomish
(360) 568-2601

Open mid-June—Oct. Berries, pumpkin patch, corn maze and special events.

Fall City Farm
3636 Neal Rd., Fall City
(425) 222-7930

Open July—Nov with U-pick produce, including garlic, apples, corn, herbs and more. Pumpkin patch and sunflower house in Oct. Tours, classes and special weekend events offered.

The Blueberry Farm
12109 Woods Creek Rd., Monroe
(360) 794-6995

Blueberry picking in July—Aug; gift shop, kids' play area, picnic tables.

Bybee-Nims Farms
42930 S.E. 92nd St., North Bend
(425) 888-0821

Open mid-July—mid-Sept with U-pick blueberries, picnic tables.

The Root Connection
13607 Woodinville-Redmond Rd., Redmond
(425) 881-1006

Open Apr—Oct, with U-pick chemical-free produce, pumpkin patch and petting zoo in Oct.

Serres Farm
20306 N.E. 50th St., Redmond
(425) 868-3017

U-pick strawberries in mid-June—July; pumpkin patch in Oct; Christmas trees (precut or cut your own) late Nov—mid-Dec.

Stocker Farms
Hwy. 9 and Marsh Rd., Snohomish
(360) 563-9619

Open June—Oct with U-pick produce, farm animals, pumpkins and corn maze.

One of the Best–Literally!
WOODLAND PARK ZOO

5500 Phinney Ave. N., Seattle
(206) 684-4800
www.zoo.org

I n the last several years, the Woodland Park Zoo has undergone extensive renovations to greatly improve its exhibits. This is one reason why this well-planned zoo has been rated one of the ten best in the United States. The Northern Trail exhibit is a good example. A multi-level showcase of lush green and rocky terrain defines the region from Alaska to Oregon. It offers ample roaming space for native grizzlies, mountain goats, eagles and wolves—while giving viewers gasp-evoking glimpses of animals at play.

Located on 92 acres, just ten minutes from downtown Seattle, the zoo boasts an impressive list of animals, from rambunctious gorillas to a pair of endangered Komodo dragons. A stroll through the grounds is an exercise in globetrotting. Stubby-legged hippos play in the African Savannah exhibit while giraffes graze nearby. Bats, raccoons and other night-eyed residents of the Nocturnal House teach visitors about life after dark. At the popular Trail of Vines exhibit, viewers stand on an observation platform high above the jungle to watch singing orangutans and siamangs.

Save an hour for the Family Farm, Habitat Discovery Trail and petting zoo if you have young kids. Outside the zoo, take a stroll through the Woodland Park rose garden adjacent to the south gate, or hit the playground outside the north gate.

Woodland Park Zoo stages numerous special events throughout the year, including a Santa Breakfast in December and a wildly popular Zoo Tunes and Zoo Tunes Jr. concert series in the summer. Pony rides for children over two are available during warm weather months. The zoo offers seminars, animal demonstrations, summer day camps, overnight programs and numerous family events. Be sure to check with the staff for upcoming events.

SEASONS AND TIMES
➤ Summer (May 1—Oct 15): Daily, 9:30 am—6 pm. Winter (Oct 16—Apr 30): Daily, 9:30 am—5 pm.

COST
➤ Adults $9, seniors $8.25, youths (6 to 17) and disabled patrons $6.50, children (3 to 5) $4.25, under 2 free. Annual family membership $50. Discounts available for King County residents.

GETTING THERE
➤ By car, from Seattle Center, head east on Mercer St. Turn north on Dexter Ave. and follow the signs onto Hwy. 99 North. Take Hwy. 99 N. to the N.E. 45th St. Exit and head west on 45th. Follow the zoo signs. There's pay parking at zoo ($3) and free parking on nearby streets. About 10 minutes from Seattle Center.
➤ By public transit, take Metro bus 5 northbound from 3rd Ave. and Pine St. downtown to the zoo's west gate at N. 55th St. and Phinney Ave. N. Call Metro Transit for schedule information (206) 553-3000.

NEARBY
➤ Fremont neighborhood, Green Lake, Woodland Park (picnic areas, walking trails, mountain biking mounds, baseball diamonds, tennis courts and soccer fields).

COMMENT
➤ Stroller rentals ($3). Bring hygienic wet-wipes for use after the petting zoo. Baby changing stations available. Plan a 2- to 3-hour visit.

Other Places to Visit

Country Village
23730 Bothell-Everett Hwy., Bothell
(425) 483-2250

This is one of the prettiest shopping centers around, with walking paths, bridges and a gazebo. Ducks and chickens wander the grounds, and rabbits and doves make their home here too. The courtyard merry-go-round and playground are perfect for toddlers. Many of the stores sell antiques and crafts; kids will most enjoy the toy store and doll hospital. Seasonal festivals are popular and include Halloween activities and Santa's arrival by sleigh in November.

Issaquah Salmon Hatchery
125 E. Sunset Way, Issaquah
(425) 392-1118

Visit the hatchery and see juvenile salmon in holding tanks and adult salmon returning to spawn. The best time to visit is September to mid-November. Open daily with self-guided tours.

Juanita Bay Park
2201 Market St., Kirkland
(425) 828-1217

Bring binoculars and search for birds and other wildlife at this wetland park. The system of trails and boardwalks is easy to navigate and interpretive signs help identify the wildlife.

Mercer Slough Nature Park
2102 Bellevue Way S.E., Bellevue
(425) 462-2752

The park is home to more than 170 species of birds, animals and amphibians living in and near the wetlands of Lake Washington. Learn about them by taking the free weekly guided nature walk. Interpretive canoe rides are offered seasonally.

Chapter 8

GREEN SPACES

Introduction

S eattle's nickname is "Emerald City" but you don't have to follow a yellow brick road to find its jewels. The city's an outdoor paradise, rich with recreational opportunities, natural wonders and awe-inspiring beauty.

On warm summer days, visit Green Lake and join the crowds enjoying the sunshine. If it's overcast or drizzling, your kids can make the most of it by jumping in puddles, watching wildlife or exploring nature in Marymoor Park. Colorful kites fly in the breeze at Gas Works Park and Sand Point Magnuson Park. Wildflowers bloom in the meadows of Discovery Park, bright red salmon return to spawn at Carkeek Park and multi-hued birds abound at Seward Park.

To see even more color, take a walk through one of the area's public gardens, such as the Woodland Park Rose Garden, Kubota Garden or Washington Park Arboretum. With these and hundreds of other green spaces, you'll never run out of new places to explore.

NOTE

Don't miss the following parks and green spaces covered elsewhere in this guide:

Outdoor Education at
CARKEEK PARK

950 N.W. Carkeek Park Rd., Seattle
(206) 684-0877
www.cityofseattle.net/parks

T his 223-acre park is a naturalist's paradise offering wetlands, beach, upland forest, meadow and riparian areas. It's also an outdoor classroom with rangers from Carkeek's environmental education center on hand daily to teach visitors about Pacific Northwest natural environments and wildlife. Carkeek's series of hiking trails are short enough for young children to manage, but can be connected to make lengthy routes for older kids. The playground boasts climbing structures, swings, artwork and a "salmon slide" that is a big hit with kids. For more fun, stand on the overpass that leads from the play area to the beach. Several times a day trains run through the park and this is the perfect spot to watch them.

Be sure to visit in November when the salmon return to spawn in Piper's Creek. Carkeek is the only park that sees a significant salmon run every year and that's due to the dedication and hard work of Carkeek-area residents. There are summer camp programs and other special events held annually. Call or visit the website for details.

SEASONS AND TIMES
➤ Year-round: Daily, 6 am—10 pm.

COST
➤ Free. Costs may apply to summer camp and special events.

GETTING THERE
➤ By car, from Seattle Center head east on Mercer St. to I-5 North.
Take the Northgate Exit off I-5 N. and go west on Northgate Way, which
turns into 105th St. Turn north onto Greenwood then west onto N.
110th St. which becomes N.W. Carkeek Park Rd. Inside the park, turn
north for the Education Center or continue straight ahead for the
trails, play and picnic areas and beach. About 15 minutes from Seattle
Center.
➤ By public transit, take Metro bus 28 heading north on 4th Ave. Get
off at 3rd Ave. N.W. and N.W. 110th. Walk west on N.W. 110th to
Carkeek Park Rd. Turn into the park. About 1 mile from the bus stop.
Can Metro Transit for route and schedule information (206) 553-3000.

NEARBY
➤ Ballard.

Active Excursions
DISCOVERY PARK

3801 W. Government Way, Seattle
(206) 386-4236
www.cityofseattle.net/parks or
www.discoveryparkfriends.org

S eattle's 534-acre Discovery Park is situated
on Magnolia Bluff overlooking Puget Sound.
It offers residents and tourists a chance to
experience pristine forest, rolling meadow, rocky

beach, spectacular cliff views and a historic military site.

Prior to 1964, Discovery Park was called Fort Lawton and belonged to the U.S. Army. Several military buildings remain above the park's South Meadow, but elsewhere Discovery is overflowing with fun things for families. If your children are active, hike Discovery's three-mile trail that boasts picnic areas and sandy cliff walks overlooking the Sound. Park rangers facilitate a wide range of nature programs (including popular Night Walks) to educate all ages about the park's history and its flora and fauna populations. The Daybreak Star Indian Cultural Center, in the northwest corner of the park, displays works by Native American artists and provides insight on local history (206-285-4425).

Trekking to South Beach and West Point is worth the effort. The beach offers some of the best tide pools around, as well as great marine bird watching and a close look at the West Point Lighthouse built in 1881. Kids can get a break from nature at the playground located behind the Visitor Center.

SEASONS AND TIMES
➤ Park: Year-round, daily, dawn—dusk. Visitor Center: Daily, 8:30 am—5 pm, closed Christmas and New Year's. Daybreak Star Indian Cultural Center: Mon—Sat, 10 am—5 pm; Sun, noon—5 pm.

COST
➤ Free. Costs may apply to summer camp programs, special events and classes.

GETTING THERE

➤ By car, from the south side of Seattle Center, head west on Denny Way. Follow it north as it becomes Western Ave. W., then Elliott Ave. W. and finally 15th Ave. W. Take the Emerson St. Exit and head west over 15th. Follow Emerson until the "T" at Gilman Way. Head north on Gilman as it turns into W. Government Way. After the 4-way stop at 34th Ave. W., the Visitor Center will be a block west on the south side. About 10 minutes from Seattle Center.

➤ By public transit, take Metro bus 33 heading northbound on 4th Ave. Call Metro Transit for route and schedule information (206) 553-3000.

NEARBY

➤ Interbay Golf Center, Ballard, Hiram M. Chittenden Locks.

Go Fly a Kite
GAS WORKS PARK

2101 N. Northlake Way, Seattle
(206) 684-4075
www.cityofseattle.net/parks

Formerly a gas plant, Gas Works Park is a unique green space in the heart of the city. Some of the old equipment remains in the boiler house that has been transformed into a picnic shelter. The exhauster-compressor building has been reborn as a children's play barn. The brightly painted machinery takes on new life as public art.

Outside, enjoy the views of the cityscape, Lake Union and the colorful kites that fill the sky above Kite Hill on breezy days. Energetic folk can take off on foot or on wheels on the Burke Gilman Trail (page 210), which starts at the park and continues 27 miles to East King County. In summer, catch free performances of Shakespeare, Seattle Peace Concerts and other live entertainment. On the Fourth of July, every inch of grass is covered with people enjoying the daylong festival that culminates with a spectacular fireworks show over Lake Union. Though the park is on the shore of the lake, no swimming, wading or boat launching is permitted. Bring a ball or a stack of books to while the day away.

SEASONS AND TIMES
➤ Park: Year-round, daily, 4 am—11:30 pm. Parking lot: Year-round, daily, 6 am—9 pm.

COST
➤ Free.

GETTING THERE
➤ By car, head east from Seattle Center on Mercer St. or Denny Way. Turn north on Dexter Ave. and continue 2 miles. Cross the Fremont Bridge. Stay in the right lane and turn east on 34th St. At Stone Way N., turn southeast onto N. Northlake Place, which becomes N. Northlake Way. About 8 minutes from Seattle Center.
➤ By public transit, take Metro bus 26 or 28 from downtown Seattle. Call Metro Transit for route and schedule information (206) 553-3000.

NEARBY
➤ University of Washington, Fremont, Woodland Park Zoo, Green Lake.

A *Jewel* in the City
GREEN LAKE

E. Green Lake Dr. N. and W. Green Lake Dr. N., Seattle
(206) 684-4075
www.cityofseattle.net/parks

More than a million visitors flock to Green Lake for recreation and relaxation each year. This urban gathering place has something for everyone, including cyclists, joggers, in-line skaters, walkers, boaters, swimmers, golfers and people-watchers too.

With a wading pool, indoor swimming pool and two swimming beaches, it's hard to stay dry at Green Lake. The beaches have lifeguards on duty in summer and offer free swimming lessons for those over six. Water quality varies; to check pollution levels call (206) 684-7080. Green Lake Boat Rentals rents canoes, paddleboats, rowboats and sailboards (no motorized craft allowed on the lake). There's also a Small Craft Center that offers boating classes and summer camps.

A paved 2.8-mile pathway that circles the lake is perfect for walking, jogging, biking and in-line skating. Other attractions include a playground, pitch and putt golf course (206-632-2280), tennis and basketball courts, soccer fields, fishing piers and picnic areas. Restaurants line the streets to the north and east of the lake. Don't miss the annual Seafair Milk Carton Derby (one Saturday in early July). Dozens of human-powered boats made of milk cartons race across the lake.

On warm weekends, the challenge of the crowds and parking make this destination difficult for families. Try visiting on a weekday or arrive early on the weekend.

SEASONS AND TIMES
→ Park: Year-round, daily. Boat rentals: Mid-Apr—Sept. Call (206) 527-0171 for hours. Pitch and putt: Mar—Oct, daily, 9 am—dusk. Evans swimming pool: Call for schedule and fees (206) 684-4961. Community center: Daily, call for current events (206) 684-0780.

COST
→ Park access: Free. Boat rentals: $10 per hour for rowboats, paddleboats, canoes and sailboards. $12 per hour for double kayaks. Pitch and putt: Adults $3.75, seniors and children $3.25.

GETTING THERE
→ By car, from Seattle Center head east on Mercer St. to I-5 North. Take I-5 N. to Exit 170 and drive about 1/2 mile northwest on Ravenna Blvd. to E. Greenlake Dr. N. Turn right (north) at the five-way stop sign and drive to the first stoplight at Lawton St. Turn south into the main parking lot, or look for street parking on adjacent streets. About 10 minutes from Seattle Center.
→ By public transit, take Metro bus 16, 26 and 48 from downtown Seattle. Call Metro Transit for route and schedule information (206) 553-3000.

NEARBY
→ Woodland Park Zoo, Fremont, University of Washington, Burke Museum.

COMMENT
→ Lock your car and don't leave valuables inside.

Wide Open Spaces
SAND POINT
MAGNUSON PARK

7400 Sand Point Way N.E., Seattle
(206) 684-4946
www.cityofseattle.net/parks/

This park encompasses 320 acres of the former Sand Point Navy base, including one mile of Lake Washington shoreline. When the Navy base closed in the 1990s, the land became part of the existing park and was renamed Sand Point Magnuson Park.

This vast green space has tons to offer families. In summer, there's always a lifeguard on duty at the swimming beach and free swimming lessons for kids over six. Younger siblings enjoy splashing about in the wading pool. Find a spot to sunbathe and watch jet skiers and wind surfers on the lake. Or, play tennis or kick a ball around on one of the sports fields. There's a hilly spot that's perfect for kite flying.

Paved trails through the park are great for bikes, trikes, scooters, skateboards and other wheeled contraptions. Blackberry bushes line the trails so bring a bucket for collecting (mid-August to September). Be sure to stop at the huge playground for some energy-burning fun. There's an off-leash dog area, interesting outdoor art to explore and the Sound Garden at the adjacent National Oceanic and Atmospheric Administration campus.

If you have extra time, visit the historic district's Art Deco and Colonial Revival buildings from the 1930s and 40s. Summer camps, after-school classes, senior programs, art installations and transitional housing are just a few of the park's new uses with many more planned.

SEASONS AND TIMES
➤ Year-round: Daily, 4 am—10 pm (until 11:30 pm, May 1—Labor Day).

COST
➤ Free.

GETTING THERE
➤ By car, from Seattle center, head east on Mercer St. to I-5 North. Take I-5 N. to the N.E. 45th St. Exit. Go east on 45th, down the 45th St. ramp as it merges into Sand Point Way N.E. Head northeast on Sand Point Way and turn east into the park entrance at N.E. 65th or 74th St. About 15 minutes from Seattle Center.
➤ By public transit, take Metro bus routes 74 or 75 from downtown and get off near either entrance along Sand Point Way N.E. Call Metro Transit for route and schedule information (206) 553-3000.

NEARBY
➤ University of Washington, University Village Shopping Center, Burke-Gilman Trail, Burke Museum.

Going Green
MARYMOOR PARK

**6046 W. Lake Sammamish Pkwy. N.E., Redmond
(206) 296-2964
www.metrokc.gov/parks/**

With over 600 acres and a lengthy list of amenities, it's no surprise that Marymoor is the most popular park in the King County Park System. People flock here for more than just a game of soccer. Among other things, Marymoor hosts several big festivals, including the Heritage Festival, Fourth of July Fireworks, WOMAD USA (page 247) and Evergreen Horse Classic.

The Marymoor Velodrome was used in the 1990 Goodwill Games and holds bike races Wednesday and Friday nights from May to September. The banked oval is open to the public at other times. Nearby, the 45-foot Marymoor Climbing Rock is a perfect for introducing youngsters to the sport of climbing.

The park's popular off-leash dog area spans 40 acres. If your kids have a green thumb, rent a plot from the park's Pea Patch and start gardening ($33 per year). For the sports-minded, there are baseball, soccer and lacrosse fields, tennis courts, a fitness circuit and a rowing facility. Nature lovers will want to walk the interpretive path through the wetlands to get a closer look at wildlife. Two regional trails are accessible as well. The Sammamish River Trail connects to the Burke-Gilman to make a 27-mile trek into Seattle, and the Bridle Crest Trail leads to Bellevue's Bridle Trails State Park.

If history is your thing, don't miss Willowmoor Farm and Clise Mansion, home to the Marymoor Museum (page 203). Finally take time to enjoy the greenery; have a picnic, fish or soak up some rays while the kids play on one of the park's two playgrounds.

SEASONS AND TIMES
➤ Year-round: Daily, 8 am—dusk.

COST
➤ Free.

GETTING THERE
➤ By car, from Seattle Center, head east on Mercer St. to I-5 North. From I-5 N., take the SR-520 E. Exit and continue on SR-520 to the W. Lake Sammamish Pkwy. N.E. Exit. Follow the signs into the park. About 20 minutes from Seattle Center.
➤ By public transit, take Metro bus route 550 from downtown Seattle to the Bellevue Transit Center and then board bus 249 to the park. Call Metro Transit for route and schedule information (206) 553-3000.

NEARBY
➤ Redmond Town Center, Farrel-McWhirter Park.

See What's Blooming
PUBLIC GARDENS

I t's not called the Emerald City for nothing. Something about the Seattle climate makes it a very fertile place for gardens. The city and its surrounding communities boast some of the best and most diverse gardens in the West. They are great places to view not only plants but also wildlife, including birds, squirrels, rabbits, heron and raccoons. Public gardens generally welcome children, are wheelchair and stroller accessible and offer basic amenities such as restrooms.

Washington Park Arboretum
2300 Arboretum Dr. E. at Lake Washington Blvd., Seattle
(206) 543-8800
www.depts.washington.edu/wpa

Pick up a map or illustrated guide to Northwest plant species. The Arboretum houses a Japanese Garden (1502 Lake Washington Blvd. E.) with stones hauled from the Cascades, and a teahouse.

University of Washington Medicinal Herb Garden
Stevens Way at Garfield Lane, Seattle
(206) 543-1126
www.nnlm.nlm.nih.gov/pnr/uwmhg

The herb garden grows the largest collection of medicinal herbs in the Western Hemisphere with more than 600 species.

Seattle Tilth Demonstration Gardens
4649 Sunnyside Ave. N., Seattle
(206) 633-0451
www.seattletilth.org

Children's garden where little green thumbs can practice organic gardening. In the family/adult garden you'll also see recycling and composting.

Kubota Garden
9817 – 55th Ave. S., Seattle (206) 725-4400
www.cityofseattle.net/parks

Established in 1927, see a dragon tree and many styles from traditional Japanese gardens.

Woodland Park Rose Garden
5500 Phinney Ave. N., Seattle
(206) 684-4863
www.zoo.org

Several hundred varieties of roses are grown here.

Bellevue Botanical Garden
12001 Main St., Bellevue
(425) 452-2750
www.bellevuebotanical.org

A series of small gardens set within 36 acres of Wilburton Hill Park.

Island Oasis
SEWARD PARK

5898 Lake Washington Blvd. S., Seattle
(206) 684-4075
www.cityofseattle.net/parks

A visit to Seward Park feels like a trip to an island—the park is situated on a peninsula jutting out into Lake Washington. This green space is a favorite for bicyclists. A two-and-one-half mile scenic, paved road encircles the peninsula and connects to the path that snakes alongside Lake Washington. The peninsula loop is an ideal place for little ones to ride without the threat of traffic.

Kids love the nautical-themed playground and the park's swimming beach (lifeguard on duty in summer). Visit the Native Plant Garden to learn about the Northwest region's plant species. Seward is also home to one of the city's few fish hatcheries where families can not only learn about fish, but also spot heron, river otters and other wildlife. Each month the Seattle Parks Department and Audubon Society offer free bird tours at the park. Hiking trails lead through the park's lush native canopy and the amphitheater is the site of community gatherings. The paths are stroller accessible so bring along your youngest to enjoy the fresh air!

SEASONS AND TIMES
➤ Year-round: Daily, 4 am–11:30 pm.

COST
➤ Free.

GETTING THERE
➤ By car, from Seattle Center, take 2nd Ave. south. Turn east onto Madison St. and continue to Lake Washington Blvd. Turn south and continue about 8 miles to the park entrance at S. Juneau St. About 20 minutes from Seattle Center.
➤ By public transit, take Metro bus 39 from 2nd Ave. to Seward Park Ave. S. and S. Orcas St. Call Metro Transit for route and schedule information (206) 553-3000.

NEARBY
➤ Kubota Garden.

Other Green Spaces

Downtown Park
10201 N.E. 4th St., Bellevue
(425) 452-6881
www.ci.bellevue.wa.us/parks

Stroll with the kids, feed ducks and enjoy well-kept grassy areas and a busy play area. Walk the half-mile circular promenade that goes around a wonderful 240-foot wide waterfall and reflecting pond below. The park is also home to Bellevue's popular outdoor ice arena during the winter holidays. This urban retreat is just one block south of Bellevue Square shopping mall.

➤ Year-round: Daily.

➤ Free. Fees apply to ice arena.

➤ From north side of Seattle Center head east on Mercer St. to I-5 South. Take I-5 S. to I-90 East. Take the I-405 N. Exit, then take the N.E. 4th St. Exit and head west. Turn south onto 100th Ave. N.E. and east into the parking lot.

Gene Coulon Memorial Beach Park

1201 Lake Washington Blvd. N., Renton
(425) 430-6700
http://ci.renton.wa.us/commserv/parks/coulon.htm

You'll find this lovely beach park at the south end of Lake Washington. Enjoy a sandy swimming beach (lifeguard in summer), playground, tennis and volleyball courts, fishing pier and an interpretive walking trail. Bring your own picnic or try the two fast food restaurants, Kidd Valley Burgers and Ivar's Fish Bar. In summer, take in a free concert on Wednesday evenings.

➛ Year-round: Daily, 7 am—dusk.

➛ From north side of Seattle Center head east on Mercer St. to I-5 South. Take I-5 S. to I-90 East. Take the I-405 S. Exit. Go to Exit 5 and head west on N.E. Park Dr. Go down the hill and turn north on to Lake Washington Blvd. The park entrance is approximately 1/4 mile further. Take Metro Transit bus 101 to S. 3rd St. and Rainier St., transfer to bus 240 and get off at Park Ave. N. and walk 3 blocks northeast to park.

City and County Parks

With hundreds of parks in the area, it's impossible to list every one. To find out more about the King County Parks System, visit www. metrokc. gov/parks or call (206) 296-4232. For information on Seattle Parks, visit www.cityofseattle. net/parks or call (206) 684-4075. Here are few suggestions; all are worth the visit.

Lincoln Park
8011 Fauntleroy Way S.W., Seattle

Forest and beach trails, sports fields and courts, picnic shelters, playgrounds, wading pool and Colman Pool—the only outdoor heated saltwater pool in Seattle (open summers only).

Jefferson Park
3801 Beacon Ave. S., Seattle

Lawn bowling, playground, sports fields and golf course.

Pratt Water Park
2000 E. Yesler Way, Seattle

Play area with water cannons and water maze. Colorful African-themed sculptures honoring slain civil rights leader Edwin T. Pratt.

Myrtle Edwards Park
3130 Alaskan Way W., Seattle

A path for bikers, walkers, joggers and in-line skaters runs along Elliott Bay. Fourth of July-Ivars festival and spectacular fireworks show.

Volunteer Park
15th Ave. E. and E. Prospect, Seattle

Climb to the top of the 75-foot water tower to get an awesome view of the city and the Sound. Visit the Conservatory in winter. The Seattle Asian Art Museum is also here (page 51).

Cougar Mountain Regional Wildland Park
18201 S.E. Cougar Mountain Dr., Issaquah

Over 3,000 acres with 36 miles of hiking trails. Interesting sites to explore including a former coal mining town, a missile site left from the Cold War, waterfalls, caves, glacial boulders, creeks and wildlife.

Luther Burbank Park
2040 – 8th Ave. S.E., Mercer Island

Off-leash area, playground, three miles of hiking trails, swimming beach, boat launch, tennis courts, picnic areas, fishing pier and an outdoor amphi-theater for summer performances.

CHAPTER 9

HISTORICAL SITES

Introduction

I t's hard for kids to imagine Seattle as anything but a big city filled with skyscrapers and traffic jams. To give them a peek at the way Seattle used to be, take them to visit one of the historical sites in this chapter.

One of the most intriguing places is Pioneer Square. Bill Speidel's Underground Tour takes visitors below street level to see storefronts and sidewalks that existed before the area was raised and rebuilt after the Great Seattle Fire of 1889. In Pioneer Square, kids can also learn about the gold rush and pan for gold at the Klondike Gold Rush National Historic Park. Nearby in the International District, you'll get a feel for a vibrant multi-cultural community that's over 100 years old.

If you like museums, don't miss the Log House Museum in West Seattle with its displays about early settlers. At the History House in Fremont, learn about Seattle's neighborhoods. Stop in at any one of a dozen community museums that offer exhibits highlighting their local lore.

At the University of Washington, explore a century's worth of higher education and see current attractions. Downtown, check out the famous Smith Tower and take a tour of the 5th Avenue Theatre. Then, head east to check out old trains at the Northwest Railway Museum and ride the Snoqualmie Railway train between May and October. Issaquah boasts two free history museums and a fabulous candy factory. With so many fun things to do, your kids won't realize the trip is educational too!

Behind the Scenes at the
5TH AVENUE THEATRE

**1308 – 5th Ave., Seattle
(206) 625-1418
www.fifthavenuetheatre.org**

Attending a show at the 5th Avenue Theatre, one can't help but marvel at its architectural design. Even with a rousing musical on stage, audience members may find themselves captivated by the theater's ornate features. While splurging on a performance for the whole family may not fit your budget, you can still get a close look at the theater by taking a free tour.

On the tour, you learn that the theater originally opened in 1926 as a vaudeville house and got its unusual Asian design because of Seattle's significance as "the gateway to the Orient." Modeled after three of ancient imperial China's greatest architectural achievements—the Forbidden City, the Temple of Heaven and the Summer Palace—the theater includes a replica of the dome in the Forbidden City's Imperial Palace. The theater closed in 1978, but was renovated and re-opened one year later through the efforts of civic-minded businesses and community leaders. Since then it has been one of the main venues for national touring shows.

SEASONS AND TIMES
➤ To request a 20-minute tour, call (206) 625-1418 weekdays between 10 am and 5 pm.

COST
➤ Free.

GETTING THERE
➤ By car, from Seattle Center, take Broad St. west to 5th Ave. Proceed south to the theater. Park on the street at metered spots or in pay parking lots. About 5 minutes from Seattle Center.
➤ By public transit, take the Monorail from Seattle Center to downtown. Walk from the Monorail terminal at Westlake Center down to street level and proceed south on 5th Ave. 2 blocks to the theater.

NEARBY
➤ Westlake Center, Pacific Place, downtown shopping core, GameWorks, Washington State Convention and Trade Center, Four Seasons Hotel.

Small-town History
HISTORIC ISSAQUAH

Visitor Information Center
155 N.W. Gilman Blvd., Issaquah
(425) 392-7024
www.issaquahhistory.org

Located at the base of the "Issaquah Alps"— Cougar, Squak and Tiger mountains—Issaquah sprang up as a coal mining town in the mid 1860s. Immigrants from many countries came to work and settled in the area. The town went through three name changes before settling on Issaquah in 1899. Prior to that it was "Gilman" and the original Gilman Town Hall still stands. It now serves as a museum (425-392-3500) with artifacts from pioneer families and an authentic old-fashioned two-cell jail.

Like many communities, the arrival of the railroad in the late 1800s expanded the town's possibilities for business and trade. The railroad's history and local significance is highlighted at the original Train Depot, which was restored in 1994 and now operates as a museum.

A more recent arrival, with its own sweet history, is Boehm's Candy Kitchen (425-392-6652). The late Julius Boehm built the candy factory in the 1950s in the style of a mountain chalet. During the summer, the shop offers free tours that include history about Boehm, an avid mountaineer who climbed Mount Everest at the age of 80, and a peek into his former living quarters. There are also candy-making demonstrations and tastings for kids.

One of the region's most unique shopping centers is in Issaquah and it exudes historical character. Gilman Village (425-392-6802) was created in the mid-1970s by a developer who acquired old buildings including farmhouses, barns and former businesses slated for demolition. He moved them to a site on Gilman Boulevard, gutted the insides but kept the facades to give 40 new shops and restaurants an old-fashioned flair. Kids will definitely enjoy White Horse Toys (425-391-1498).

SEASONS AND TIMES
➤ Visitor Information Center: Mon—Fri, 9 am—5 pm; Sat—Sun,

10 am—4 pm.
Gilman Town Hall Museum: Thu and Sat, 11 am—3 pm. Train Depot:
Sat, 11 am—4 pm. Gilman Village: Mon—Wed, 10 am—6 pm; Thu—Fri,
10 am—8 pm; Sat, 10 am—6 pm; Sun, 11 am—5 pm. Boehm's Candy
Kitchen: Mon—Sat, 9 am—6 pm; Sun, 11 am—6 pm. Call ahead to
reserve a tour.

GETTING THERE

➤ By car, from Seattle Center head east on Mercer St. to I-5 South.
Take I-5 S. to the I-90 E. Exit. Continue on I-90 E. to Exit 17 (Front
St.) and head south. Go east on Gilman Blvd. to Boehm's Candy
Kitchen (255 N.E. Gilman Blvd.). Go west on Gilman to the Visitor
Information Center and Gilman Village (317 N.W. Gilman Blvd.).
Proceed south on Front St. to Gilman Town Hall Museum (2 blocks
east of Front St. at 165 S.E. Andrews St.), Historic Railroad Depot
Museum (1 block east of Front St. in Depot Park at 50 Rainier Blvd.
N.), and old downtown. About 30 minutes from Seattle Center.
➤ By public transit, take Metro bus routes 210, 214 or 215 to the
Issaquah Park & Ride then take bus 200 into downtown Issaquah. Call
Metro Transit for route and schedule information (206) 553-3000.

COST

➤ Free admission to all attractions noted.

NEARBY

➤ Lake Sammamish State Park, Snoqualmie Falls, Cougar Mountain
Zoo, Issaquah Alps, Issaquah Salmon Hatchery, Pickering Place,
Village Theatre, Illusions Magical Entertainment Center.

COMMENT

➤ Plan an all-day visit.

What's in Your Neighborhood?
HISTORY HOUSE

790 N. 34th, Seattle
(206) 675-8875
www.scn.org/neighbors/historyhouse

There are over 90 neighborhoods in Seattle. The unique history of each tells part of the story of Seattle's evolution from a seaside-fishing town to major metropolis. History House, located in the Fremont neighborhood, is the place to find out about the not-so-famous people and places that made Seattle what it is today. In fact, the creation of History House was an unofficial invitation for longtime Seattle families to go through their attics and contribute artifacts and photographs from the past.

History House provides an excellent stepping-stone for youngsters to become interested in Seattle's roots. The museum offers numerous inter-active displays, videos and hands-on activities that will teach school age children about the arts, technology and humanities of Seattle's varied and vibrant neighborhoods.

SEASONS AND TIMES
➤ Year-round: Wed—Sun, noon—5 pm.

COST

➤ Suggested donation $1.

GETTING THERE

➤ By car, from Seattle Center, head east on Mercer St. until Dexter Ave. Turn north and continue about 2 miles to the Fremont Bridge. Stay in the right lane after crossing the bridge and head east on 34th St. Street parking. About 10 minutes from Seattle Center.

➤ By public transit, take Metro bus 28 from downtown Seattle to Fremont hub and walk east on N. 34th to the museum. Call Metro Transit for route and schedule information (206) 553-3000.

NEARBY

➤ Fremont neighborhood, Green Lake, Ballard, Hiram Chittenden Locks, Gas Works Park, Burke Gilman Trail, Woodland Park Zoo.

COMMENT

➤ Plan a 1- to 2-hour visit.

A *Fusion of Cultures*
INTERNATIONAL DISTRICT

Between 5th St., 8th St., S. Washington St. and S. Dearborn St., Seattle

Nearly 100 years ago, the International District was built on reclaimed tide flats south of downtown Seattle by the waterfront. It is the only place in the continental U.S. where Chinese, Japanese, Filipinos, African Americans and Vietnamese have built a shared community.

Chinatown was first established along King Street, followed by Nihonmachi (Japantown) near Main Street. Japanese businesses disappeared when their owners were sent to internment camps during

World War II. Filipinos and African Americans next settled into the area. The district deteriorated in the early 1970s but has been revitalized in recent years. It is now home to businesses, restaurants and cultural centers. During the July Seafair festivities, the community hosts a lively summer festival and an annual Chinatown parade.

To learn more about the area's history, stop by the Wing Luke Asian Museum (page 54) to see the displays and pick up a free walking tour brochure. One of the highlights you won't want to miss is the International Children's Park (7th Ave. S. and S. Lane St.). Also look for the bronze dragon and the China Gate restaurant (514-518 7th Ave. S.) built in 1924 as a Chinese Opera House. Then check out the Higo Variety Store (602-608 S. Jackson St.), one of the few pre-World War II Japanese American businesses still in operation, and Hing Hay Park (Maynard Ave. S. and S. King St.). Uwajimaya, a large Asian grocery and gift store is a must-see. It is part of the new Uwajimaya Village, a shopping and residential center (600 – 6th Ave. S; 206-624-6248).

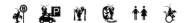

SEASONS AND TIMES
➤ Year-round: Daily.

GETTING THERE
➤ By car, from Seattle Center, head east on Mercer St. to I-5 South. Take 1-5 S. and exit at Dearborn St. Drive west toward Safeco Field. Turn north on 7th or 8th. Park at a pay lot or on the street. About 10 minutes from Seattle Center.
➤ By public transit, board any southbound bus at the Seattle bus tunnel (downtown at Westlake Center). Get off at the International District station and walk east. Call Metro Transit for route and schedule information (206) 553-3000.

NEARBY
Safeco Field, Pioneer Square, downtown Seattle.

COMMENT
Plan at least a 2-hour visit. Stop at Uwajimaya and other shops, parks
and restaurants.

Going for Gold
KLONDIKE GOLD RUSH
NATIONAL HISTORICAL
PARK

117 S. Main St., Seattle
(206) 553-7220
www.nps.gov/klse/

You may not find any gold, but planning a visit
to the Klondike Gold Rush National Historical Park will definitely enrich your lives.

The Seattle facility is one of two national regis-
tered parks in North America focusing on the Gold
Rush. You will learn how the quest for gold helped
build cities throughout the Northwest. From 1897 to
1898 for example, tens of thousands of people from
around the world descended upon Seattle's commercial district in search of equipment, pack animals,
food and clothing to use in their search for riches.

Klondike Historical Park employs an array of
media to tell the hopeful (more often woeful) miners'
tales—including antique photographs and maps,
films, narration and slide shows. Real equipment,

such as shovels, picks, clothes and pans the gold-diggers used, are a big hit with kids. Warning: take in the panning demonstration at your own risk! Once your kids learn how panning was done, your backyard may become new Klondike Yukon Territory.

SEASONS AND TIMES
➤ Year-round: Daily, 9 am—5 pm. Closed Thanksgiving, Christmas and New Year's.

COST
➤ Free.

GETTING THERE
➤ By car, from south side of Seattle Center, head south on 1st Ave. Turn east onto Main. Street parking is available and free Sundays and holidays. About 10 minutes from Seattle Center.
➤ By public transit, Pioneer Square is serviced by several Metro bus routes. The Waterfront Streetcar also stops here. Call Metro Transit for route and schedule information (206) 553-3000.

COMMENT
➤ Plan a 1-hour visit.

NEARBY
➤ Waterfront, ferries, Pioneer Square (restaurants), Pike Place Market, Safeco Field, Seattle Art Museum, Seattle Metropolitan Police Museum.

Seattle's Birthplace
LOG HOUSE MUSEUM

3003 − 61st Ave. S.W., West Seattle
(206) 938-5293
www.loghousemuseum.org

T he history of the founding of Seattle is short but colorful. Nowhere is it told better than at the city's birthplace—an authentically renovated log house circa the 1850s. Known as the Log House Museum and operated by the Southwest Seattle Historical Society, this unique place uses artifacts, videos, old photographs and information panels to tell stories of the early inhabitants of the area. It recently opened The Spirit Returns: A Duwamish and Pioneer Story. This interactive display recounts the history of the beachfront area where Seattle's first settlers landed and the indigenous Duwamish welcomed them as neighbors.

The museum also sponsors a children's reading hour, lectures, a traveling history show and other special events.

SEASONS AND TIMES
→ Year-round: Thu, noon—6 pm; Fri, 10 am—3 pm; Sat—Sun, noon—3 pm.

COST
→ Suggested donation: Adults $2, children $1.

GETTING THERE
➤ By car, from Seattle Center, head east on Mercer St. to I-5 South. Take I-5 S. to Exit 163 (Spokare St./ West Seattle Bridge) and head west over the bridge. Take the Admiral Way Exit and head north and then west on Admiral for 2 miles. Turn south on 61st Ave. S.W. About 20 minutes from Seattle Center.

NEARBY
➤ Alki Beach, Luna Café, West Seattle ferry terminal.

COMMENT
➤ Plan a 1- to 2-hour visit.

Working on the Railroad
NORTHWEST RAILWAY MUSEUM

38625 S.E. King St., Snoqualmie
(425) 888-3030
www.trainmuseum.org

A t this free museum, visitors can view one of the largest collections of railway equipment in the U.S. There are lots of large items on display, including steam locomotives, passenger and freight cars, a rotary snowplow, an Army ambulance kitchen car and track maintenance equipment. Smaller artifacts for viewing in the historic depot include dining car china, lanterns, signs and specialized tools and equipment.

The museum owns and operates a five-and-a-half-mile interpretive railway that runs between

Snoqualmie and North Bend on weekends, April through October. The highlight for kids is the special Santa Train, which runs in December. The School Train functions as an educational program for students and teaches train safety and railroad history. Adults who want to experience railroading first hand can learn how to be conductors, engineers, brakemen and firemen. Then they can assist in the interpretive railway as volunteers.

SEASONS AND TIMES
→ Memorial Day—late Sept: Daily, 11 am—7 pm. Early Oct—Memorial Day: Thu—Mon, 10 am—5 pm.

COST
→ Free.

GETTING THERE
→ By car, from Seattle Center, head east on Mercer St. to I-5 South. Take I-5 S. to the I-90 E. Exit. Take I-90 east to Exit 27. Follow the signs to downtown Snoqualmie. The Railway Museum is at Snoqualmie Depot at the south side of the intersection of King St. and Railroad Ave. About 45 minutes from Seattle Center.

NEARBY
→ Snoqualmie Falls, North Bend, Issaquah.

COMMENT
→ Plan 30 minutes to visit the museum and another hour for riding the train.

The City Below the City
PIONEER SQUARE AND UNDERGROUND TOUR

Doc Maynard's Public House
610 First Ave., Seattle
(206) 682-4646
www.undergroundtour.com

There are plenty of reasons to visit historic Pioneer Square, Seattle's first commercial district. It's home to some of the city's oldest buildings, best art galleries and most popular eateries. There's also the Annual Pioneer Square Fire Festival and parade, First Thursday Gallery Walk (where art galleries throw open their doors for free viewings) and the annual Fat Tuesday Mardi Gras celebration. If you love books, you have to stop in at Elliott Bay Bookstore (101 Main St.; 206-624-6600) — one of Seattle's very best. And you can't help but get swept up in the sports fever that accompanies the Mariners or Seahawks games at the nearby stadiums. The biggest lure for kids, however, is Bill Speidel's Underground Tour.

The tour leads visitors beneath the streets of Pioneer Square for a glimpse of turn-of-the-century storefronts and sidewalks. These were created when Seattle street levels were raised from between 8 and 35 feet following the Great Seattle Fire of 1889. The underground shops were abandoned in the early 1900s. The dark, subterranean streets are fascinating and a little frightening. Wander through underground tunnels, look at old shop equipment and forgotten sidewalks or peek up through skylights at the underside of the sidewalks above.

Pioneer Square is also home to Smith Tower (page 199), the Grand Central Bakery (214 – 1st Ave. S.; 206-622-3644) and a great family store, Magic Mouse Toys (603 – 1st Ave.; 206-682-8097).

SEASONS AND TIMES
➤ Pioneer Square: Year-round, daily. Underground tour: Sat, 1 pm, 2 pm and 3 pm; Sun, 1 pm, 2 pm and 4 pm. Other times available. Call for a schedule or to reserve.

COST
➤ Pioneer Square: Free. Underground tour: Adults $8, seniors and students (13 to 17) $7, children (7 to 12) $4, under 7 free.

GETTING THERE
➤ By car, from south side of Seattle Center, go 1 block west on Denny Way to 1st Ave. Head south on 1st to Pioneer Square. Metered parking on the street. About 6 minutes from Seattle Center.
➤ By public transit, most southbound buses on 1st Ave. run to Pioneer Square. Call Metro Transit for route and schedule information (206) 553-3000.

NEARBY
➤ Smith Tower, Waterfront, Downtown Seattle, Waterfront Trolley, International District, Seattle Aquarium, Washington State Ferries, Klondike Gold Rush National Park, Seattle Metropolitan Police Museum.

COMMENT
➤ The site is partially accessible to wheelchairs and strollers. Plan a 2-hour visit, longer with the tour.

Towering Tall
SMITH TOWER

**500 - 2nd Ave., Seattle
(206) 622-4004**

At a height of 42 stories (522 feet), Smith Tower was once the tallest building in Seattle. In fact, when it was built in 1914, it was the tallest building west of the Mississippi River. The tower was the main icon and the city's point of reference until the Space Needle was built in the 1960s.

From the observation deck on the 35th floor, enjoy panoramic views of the city, the Cascade and Olympic mountain ranges. Check out the Chinese Room, an elegant ballroom decorated in works of art from the 17th Century. Furnishings made of imported Chinese Blackwood are intricately carved by hand. Ceiling panels relate the history of Washington, Alaska and Seattle. Ask one of the employees to translate as the story is told in Chinese characters. Smith Tower may not be the most exciting historical hotspot it Seattle, but it is one of the originals. Help you kids use their imagination—by picturing how different the view would have been from the top at the turn of the century.

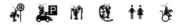

SEASONS AND TIMES
➤ Open seasonally, call for a schedule.

COST
➤ Observation deck: Adults $4, seniors, students with ID and children (6 to 12) $2.

GETTING THERE
➤ By car, head south on 2nd Ave. crossing Denny Way, for about 1 mile. Smith Tower is at the corner of 2nd and Yesler Way. Park in triangle lot on 2nd and Yesler across from the Tower. About 10 minutes from Seattle Center.
➤ By public transit, catch any southbound bus on 1st, 2nd or 3rd avenues and get off at Yesler Way in Pioneer Square. Call Metro Transit for route and schedule information (206) 553-3000.

NEARBY
➤ Pioneer Square, Klondike Gold Rush National Park, Waterfront and ferry terminals, Seattle Metropolitan Police Museum, International District.

COMMENT
➤ Plan a 1-hour visit.

A *History Lesson*
UNIVERSITY OF WASHINGTON

Visitor Information Center
4014 University Way N.E., Seattle
(206) 543-9198
http://depts.washington.edu/visitors

F amilies can learn a lot at the University of Washington (UW), even before the kids are enrolled. The school's Fisheries Department operates a salmon hatchery, releasing baby salmon into Lake Washington every year. The campus is also home to flocks of ducks, geese and pigeons, all hankering for a hand-out at Drumweller fountain. And for an in-town picnic under the blossoming cherry trees in spring, UW campus can't be beat.

For the more scientific or history-oriented, take a tour of campus to learn why the elaborately carved figures adorning the Suzzalo Library at UW look so familiar (they include some of the most famous minds in human history). Among other interesting tidbits, you'll also find out what those brick towers in the University's Red Square are for.

If you'd rather stare back in time, spend an evening at the Campus Observatory. It boasts one of the oldest telescopes in the west. A visit to the Burke Museum (page 39) is always a delight with its dinosaur relics and ancient Native American artifacts. In certain seasons, you may find works of art created by students displayed in trees and on walkways throughout the campus.

For more trees, check out the university's forestry department that is home to more than 80 species (find a tour online at www.washington.edu/home/treetour/). Be sure to investigate the medicinal garden, one of the most extensive in the region, and Washington Park Arboretum (page 176), which was established by the university and the City of Seattle in 1934.

SEASONS AND TIMES
➤ Campus tours: Year-round, daily starting at 10:30 am. Tours originate at Visitor Information Center. Observatory: Year-round, Mon—Thu evenings, weather permitting. Viewing times season dependent. Call for details (206-543-0126). Hatchery tours: Mon, Wed, Fri in the fall. Call for times (206-684-7624).

COST
➤ Free.

GETTING THERE
➤ By car, from Seattle Center, head east on Mercer St. to I-5 North. Take 1-5 N. and get off at 45th St./University of Washington Exit. Head east on N.E. 45th St. The entrance to the University is located the corner of 17th Ave. N.E. and N.E. 45th St. Parking lots are located throughout campus ($3 to $6). About 10 minutes from Seattle Center.
➤ By public transit, more than a dozen Metro routes serve the University District including 7, 25, 43, 45, 66, 70, 71, 72, 73, 74, 76, 79, 83, 377. Call Metro Transit for route and schedule information (206) 553-3000.

NEARBY
➤ University District, Wallingford, Ravenna Park, Husky Stadium, Gas Works Park, Museum of History & Industry, Burke Museum.

COMMENTS
➤ Spring and fall are the best times to visit when the campus is in full color. Plan a 1- to 2-hour visit.

Other Historical Sites

Many towns in the greater Seattle area have their own historical museums with exhibits chronicling local lore. Most are located in historical buildings and offer free or low-cost admission ($1 to $2). Here are some to explore. Since often staffed by volunteers, hours and days may change. Please call ahead to confirm.

BLACK DIAMOND HISTORICAL MUSEUM
32627 Railroad Ave., Black Diamond
(360) 886-2142
➤ Thu, 9 am—3 pm; Sat—Sun, noon—3 pm.

BLACKMAN HOUSE MUSEUM/PIONEER VILLAGE
118 Ave. B, Snohomish
(360) 568-5235
➤ Wed—Sun, noon—4 pm.

BOTHELL HISTORICAL MUSEUM
9919 N.E. 180th St., Bothell
(425) 486-1889
➤ Sun, 1—4 pm.

EDMONDS HISTORICAL MUSEUM
118 – 5th Ave. N., Edmonds
(425) 774-0900
➤ Wed—Sun, 1—4 pm.

MARYMOOR MUSEUM
6046 West Lake Sammamish Parkway N.E.
Clise Mansion in Marymoor Park, Redmond
(425) 885-3684
www.marymoormuseum.org
➤ Tue—Thu, 11am—4 pm; Sat—Sun, 1—4 pm.

RENTON HISTORICAL MUSEUM
235 Mill Ave. S., Renton
(425) 255-2330
➤ Tue, 9 am—4 pm; Wed—Sun, 1—4 pm.

SHORELINE HISTORICAL MUSEUM
749 N. 175th St., Shoreline
(206) 542-7111
➤ Tue—Sat, 10 am—4 pm.

SNOQUALMIE VALLEY HISTORICAL MUSEUM
320 North Bend Blvd. S., North Bend
(425) 888-3200
➤ Thu—Sun, 1—5 pm.

SNOHOMISH COUNTY MUSEUM AND HISTORICAL ASSOCIATION
2817 Rockefeller Ave., Everett
(425) 259-2022
➤ Wed—Sat, 1—4 pm.

WHITE RIVER VALLEY MUSEUM
918 H St. S.E., Auburn
(253) 939-2590
➤ Wed—Sun, noon—4 pm.

WINTERS HOUSE
2102 Bellevue Way S.E., Bellevue
(425) 452-2752
➤ Mon—Sat, 10 am—4 pm; Sun, noon—4 pm.

CHAPTER 10

GETTING THERE IS HALF THE FUN

Introduction

A ride on a Washington State Ferry is a relaxing, quick way to get to the mountains and beaches, and an adventure in itself if you have children. A car-toting ferry, with its colorful lifeboats and huge wind-blown decks, is often the best part of the trip—especially for kids.

Want to learn about the city in a unique way? Hitch a ride on a Ride the Ducks Tour. These amphibious land-yachts offer open-air touring in a vehicle that moves seamlessly from land to water.

For train lovers, *Amtrak Cascades* offers service to cities north and south of Seattle. For an upscale ride, check out the *Spirit of Washington Dinner Train*. It features fine scenery, great food and the hum and roll of a big train—and for part of the year, kids ride and eat free. Young children may find the Snoqualmie Valley Railroad more their pace, especially if you've managed to score them a seat on the popular *Santa Train* in December.

For something a little different, climb aboard a seaplane. A 20-minute tour by air gives passengers a taste of Seattle from new heights. Longer tours showcase Mount Rainier and Mount St. Helens.

Getting there doesn't have to be a big production. Something as simple as traveling around the city on public transportation is often a thrill for youngsters. Self-propelled transportation, including bikes and boats, is yet another way to get a different view of the city—and some exercise besides!

All Aboard!
AMTRAK CASCADES

King Street Station, 303 S. Jackson St., Seattle
1-800-USA-RAIL
www.AmtrakCascades.com

Forget the bus; forget the car; forget the plane. If you want an adventure that's exciting, educational and inexpensive, head downtown to the Seattle Amtrak station. A ride on the *Amtrak Cascades* north to Vancouver B.C., or south to Portland, Oregon, is more relaxing than driving and more fun for the kids.

The excitement starts as soon as your family steps onto the platform. Youngsters love watching the big engines pull into the station. Once aboard, kids can walk from car to car, visit the snack bar and watch the ever-changing scenery out the window. If you're taking a longer trek, Amtrak offers family-friendly movies to keep the kids from asking, "Are we there yet?"

If you can't spare more than a few hours, ride the rails to nearby cities like Everett, Tacoma or Olympia, the state's capitol. Check out Forest Park in Everett (page 146), Point Defiance Zoo and Aquarium in Tacoma (page 150), or Capitol Campus and monuments in Olympia. No matter what your destination, consider bringing the family bikes. Bikes increase the cost of a ticket $5 each way, but make getting around your destination town easy and fun.

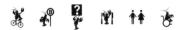

SEASONS AND TIMES
➤ Trains: Year-round, daily. Ticket counter: Daily, 6:15 am—8 pm.

COST
➤ Varies. Seattle to Tacoma round-trip: Adults around $25 each, children $12 each.

GETTING THERE
➤ By car, from Seattle Center, head east on Mercer St. to I-5 South. Take I-5 S. to the Madison St. Exit and head west on Madison. Turn south on 5th Ave. to S. Jackson (at Yesler, 5th begins to curve southwest). Turn and head west on S. Jackson for 1 block. The station is 2 blocks down on the south side of the street. About 8 minutes from Seattle Center.

NEARBY
➤ Safeco Field, Pioneer Square, Columbia Tower, International District, Ferry Terminals, Klondike Gold Rush National Park, Seattle Metropolitan Police Museum.

COMMENT
➤ Baby changing station on trains. Plan at least a half-day outing.

Fresh Air and a Workout
PEDAL, PADDLE, SKATE
OR WALK

Despite its often cloudy and damp climate, Seattle is home to many active and outdoorsy folks. With handy trails for biking, walking and roller-skating and an abundance of lakes for paddling all manner of watercraft, it's easy and fun to "get physical." Here are some destinations for self-propelled family outings with equipment rentals available nearby. Besides the health benefits, it's refreshing to get a different perspective on places you've only seen from a distance by car.

Paddling Lake Union

Gain awesome views of the city skyline, get close enough to touch houseboats, take a shore break at Gasworks Park or Ivar's Salmon House, see the ancient ferry *Kalakala*, and cruise by big yachts and speed boats. Rent boats at these locations on Lake Union:

AGUA VERDE PADDLE CLUB
(kayaks)
1303 N.E. Boat St., Seattle
(206) 545-8570
www.aguaverde.com

CENTER FOR WOODEN BOATS
(rowboats and sailboats)
1010 Valley St., Seattle
(206) 382-2628
www.cwb.org

MOSS BAY ROWING AND KAYAK CENTER
(kayaks, canoes and sailboats)
Yale St. Marina, 1001 Fairview Ave. N., Seattle
(206) 682-2031
www.mossbay.net

NW OUTDOOR CENTER
(kayaks)
2100 Westlake Ave. N., Suite 1, Seattle
(206) 281-9694
www.nwoc.com

Paddling Lake Washington

Explore the Arboretum and Foster Island by boat. You can rent from the above listed locations on Lake Union (plan to be out at least an hour or two if you do) or at the University of Washington on Lake Washington.

UNIVERSITY OF WASHINGTON
(canoes and rowboats)
Waterfront Activities Center
Off Montlake Blvd., Seattle
(206) 543-9433

Burke-Gilman/
Sammamish River Trail

This 27-mile paved trail goes from Gasworks Park on south Lake Union, up and around the north end of Lake Washington, all the way to Marymoor Park in Redmond. You don't have to go that far! Rent skates across from Gas Works Park or ride a bike (rentals near University Village, just north of the University of Washington) or just walk and push a stroller.

URBAN SURF
(in-line skates)
2100 N. Northlake Way, Seattle
(206) 545-9463

BICYCLE CENTER
4529 Sandpoint Way N.E., Seattle
(206) 523-8300

Going Public
BUSES, STREETCARS
AND MONORAIL

**King County Department of Transportation, Seattle
(206) 553-3000 (information), (206) 287-8463 (schedule)
http://transit.metrokc.gov**

I f you want to see the town for the price of a no-frills breakfast, Metro, Seattle-King County's mass transit system, is for you. The region's public transportation network will get you anywhere you want to go at low or, in the case of downtown Seattle's Ride Free Area, no cost. Metro bus and Waterfront Streetcar schedules can be obtained from Metro's website or at the number listed above. Exact change is helpful when buying a ticket. Be sure to take a ticket if you plan to transfer or ride back. Tickets are valid on all Metro transit for an hour after purchase. Bikes are welcome as most buses are equipped with bike racks. The Seattle Center Monorail's two-minute ride provides speedy, fun transportation between downtown Seattle and Seattle Center.

Metro Bus

Buses are available on most major streets in Seattle and on many of the smaller roads. To find your way around town, just call the Metro information line and tell the operator where you are and where you want to go. If you are bussing downtown, check out Seattle's 1.3-mile bus tunnel that features colorful murals, clocks, electronic art and etched tiles. The tunnel, part of the Ride Free Area, boasts more fire and police safety systems than most banks.

Waterfront Streetcar, Metro Route 99

Despite the Waterfront Streetcar's antique look, the 1927 Australian streetcars were in fact brought to Seattle from Melbourne in 1982. Waterfront Streetcars roll between Myrtle Edwards Park, through Pioneer Square, and the International District. Hop off to visit Safeco Field, Elliott Bay Book Company or the new football stadium; these are some of the many attractions within walking distance of the Streetcar route. The Streetcar is not part of the Ride Free Area.

Monorail

Built for the 1962 World's Fair, the Monorail is a fast light-rail train that runs two stories above 5th Avenue between Seattle Center and Westlake Center. It's a huge hit with kids and a great way to move from the city's festival core at Seattle Center to downtown. Contact (206) 441-6038 or www.seattlemonorail.com for more information.

SEASONS AND TIMES

➤ Metro Buses: Daily. Call for exact times. Tunnel: Mon—Fri, 5 am—7 pm; Sat, 10 am—6 pm. Closed Sundays and holidays. Ride Free Zone (from Battery St. to Jackson St. and 6th Ave. to the waterfront): Daily, 6 am—7 pm. Waterfront Streetcar: Mon—Fri, 6:45 am—7 pm; Sat—Sun, 10 am—7 pm. Monorail: Mon—Fri, 7:30 am—11 pm; Sat—Sun, 9 am—11 pm.

COST

➻ Bus and Streetcar—Single Ticket (one zone): Adults $1 (off hours) and $1.25 (peak hours), youths (5 to 17) $0.75, under 5 free. Monthly passes (one zone): Adults $45, youths (5 to 17) $27. Monorail (one-way): Adults $1.25, seniors, students and children (5 to 11) $0.50. Double fare round-trip. Group discounts and monthly passes available.

COMMENT

➻ Give yourself extra time to get to your destination. Peak commuting hours are weekdays, 6 am to 9 am and 3 pm to 6 pm. Metro's Zone One fare covers destinations within Seattle City Limits. For destinations outside city limits or for some parts of unincorporated King County, the more expensive Zone Two fare will apply.

A *Quacking Good Time*
RIDE THE DUCKS

5th St. and Broad St., Seattle
(206) 441-DUCK
www.ridetheducksofseattle.com

If being something of a public spectacle and listening to duck-inspired music sounds are painful to you, you'll want to skip this outing. But if you want to get a "duck's eye" view of the city, travel on land and water in the same vehicle, flap your arms like a duck, make noises through a yellow-lipped "Wacky Quacker" and dance and sing to blaring disco tunes, then you're bound to get a kick out of Ride the Ducks.

The entertainment factor for kids is unbeatable— it's a city tour like no other. The driver's narration is peppered with jokes, silly antics and some interesting tidbits of Seattle lore. The amphibious motor vehicles you ride in—named DUKW by the government—were built mainly by women for World War II military use. Their water-worthiness is put to the test in Lake Union, where the tour floats past houseboats, the ferry *Kalakala*, Ivar's Salmon House and marinas. Other highlights include downtown Seattle, the waterfront, the Aurora Bridge and Fremont. Let loose, act like a kid and have a ducky good time on this wacky ride.

SEASONS AND TIMES

➛ Summer (Memorial Day—Labor Day): Daily, 9:30 am—7 pm. Winter: Daily, 11:30 am—5 pm.

COST

➛ Adults $20, children $10.

GETTING THERE

➛ By car, from I-5 take the Mercer St. Exit and head west towards the Space Needle. Buy tickets at the kiosk next to the Space Needle, then walk across 5th Ave. to the boarding spot. Some free parking is available on nearby streets. During special events, parking fees at Center parking lots are based on the number of people in the vehicle. Expect to pay between $6 and $12 for all-day parking.

➛ By public transit, more than a dozen Metro routes service Seattle Center, which is across the street. Call Metro Transit for route and schedule information (206) 553-3000. Or take the Monorail that travels between Seattle Center and downtown Seattle's Westlake Center.

NEARBY

➛ Seattle Center, downtown Seattle, Pike Place Market, waterfront.

COMMENT

➛ The tour is 90 minutes long. Reservations are recommended but walk-ups are also welcome.

Giddy-up Around Town
SEALTH HORSE CARRIAGES

**Westlake Center (Pine St. between 4th and 5th Avenues)
and along the Waterfront (between Pier 55 and the
Seattle Aquarium on Alaskan Way), Seattle
(425) 277-8282
www.bcity.com/heavyhorse**

There was a time when riding in a horse-drawn carriage was the only way to get around Seattle. Today, families have endless transportation options, but none as regal as a ride in a Sealth Tours' horse-drawn carriage.

Trotting along the waterfront, through Pioneer Square or out-and-about downtown near Westlake Center—your kids will love the clip-clopping of the horses' hooves and waving to passing pedestrians. Drivers are happy to share tidbits of city history and can recommend fun places and restaurants to visit.

During the winter months, horse carriages are part of Seattle's festive holiday decor. On cold nights, snuggle up with the little ones under traditional patterned wool blankets and parkas. Carriages are equipped with convertible weatherproof tops, ready for Seattle's frequent showers.

Most horses are friendly and welcome a pat on the nose (ask the driver first!). If you want to make your child's birthday extra special, invite a few of his or her friends and reserve a carriage beforehand.

Make it an afternoon to remember and have the carriage drop you off at a downtown location for cake and ice cream.

SEASONS AND TIMES
➤ Year-round: Fri—Tue, 2 pm—10 pm. Reservations welcome but not necessary.

COST
➤ Tours (30 and 60 minutes): $40 and $80 (per carriage, holds 4 to 6 people). Champagne and Roses Tour: $80 to $200. Credit cards accepted.

GETTING THERE
➤ Westlake Center: From Seattle Center take the Monorail to Westlake Center or walk along 4th Ave. to Stewart St. Sealth carriages can be found on Pine St. between 4th Ave. and 5th Ave.
➤ Waterfront: Go west on Denny Way on the south side of Seattle Center and head south on Western Ave. Go west on Broad and veer south onto Alaskan Way. Sealth carriages can be found lined up between Pier 55 and the Seattle Aquarium on Alaskan Way. About 5 minutes from Seattle Center.
➤ By public transit, take any downtown bus headed south from Seattle Center. Walk west to 1st Ave. to get down to the Waterfront via the Pike Place Hill Climb or Harbor Steps.

NEARBY
➤ Pioneer Square, downtown Seattle, Waterfront, Seattle Center, Myrtle Edwards Park, Westlake Center, Safeco Field, Seattle Art Museum, Benaroya Hall.

COMMENT
➤ 1/2- to 1-hour visit.

Flying High
SEATTLE SEAPLANES

**1325 Fairview Ave. E., Seattle
(206) 329-9638 or 1-800-637-5553 (toll free)
www.seattleseaplanes.com**

For a unique approach to the city's main attractions, a 20-minute tour of Seattle via seaplane can't be beat. The plane takes off from the south end of Lake Union and makes a wide circular tour. A map given to each passenger shows points of interest; some are well off in the distance while others are right below. Especially notable from overhead is the University of Washington campus with its historic buildings, Red Square and fountain and Husky Stadium. There is a fly-by of Bill Gates' house on Lake Washington, then a good look at downtown Seattle's skyscrapers and the waterfront.

Next, it's over the water along the shores of Magnolia and Discovery Park, a quick peek at the Locks, the greenery of Woodland Park Zoo, ant-sized people traversing the trail around the waters of Green Lake and a glance down at Gas Works Park. The ride concludes with a calm landing back on Lake Union.

Moving at speeds of 125 miles per hour, the seaplane covers a lot more area than a car or bus in the same amount of time, but with much less detail. It's an expensive way to see the city, but for a special occasion it's quite a treat for kids.

SEASONS AND TIMES
➤ Weather-dependent. Call ahead for reservations.

COST
➤ 20-minute tour of Seattle: $42.50 per person (5 passenger maximum). Flights also available to Mt. St. Helens, Mt. Rainier, Victoria and the San Juan Islands.

GETTING THERE
➤ By car from Seattle Center, go east on Denny Way then turn north on Fairview. Stay in the right lane as Fairview veers to the northeast after the Mercer St. I-5 ramps, then proceed several blocks to the Seattle Seaplanes sign on the lake side. Free parking. About 5 minutes from Seattle Center.
➤ By public transit, take Metro bus 70 north from downtown Seattle and get off on Fairview Ave. N., across from Seattle Seaplanes.

NEARBY
➤ Seattle Center, downtown Seattle, Gas Works Park, Fremont, University of Washington.

COMMENT
➤ Call to reserve your seat at least 24 hours in advance. If your kids are prone to motion sickness, be sure to have them take some motion sickness pills beforehand.

Yes! That is a Beetle!
SPACE NEEDLE

Seattle Center, Seattle
(206) 905-2100
www.spaceneedle.com

There are a number of reasons to put the Space Needle on your itinerary. The most obvious for adults is the panoramic view from the top, but the ride up is what kids love best.

Hop into one of the Needle's "Beetles," a shimmery glass elevator for a 60-second zip up the tower. The ride is quick but the elevator hosts pack a lot of Seattle history into that minute. Once at the top, peek through binoculars on the observation deck to pick out Seattle landmarks. Head inside and watch diners in the revolving restaurant. The meals are expensive for families, but if you opt to dine, try to pick a window seat. Kids get a huge kick out of placing a penny on the railing that rings the restaurant, watching it disappear and then reappear later.

Don't forget to keep an eye out for the Sneedle. Local lore maintains that this smaller, cuddlier version of the Needle arose from the leftover building materials piled in a nearby maintenance shed during the construction of the Needle. For more lore, check the gift shop for the book *The Wheedle on the Needle*.

Be sure to pack something warm; it can get chilly at the top. Pick a day when the sun is shining for an optimal view of the surroundings.

SEASONS AND TIMES
➤ Observation deck: Year-round, Sun—Thu, 9 am—11 pm; Fri—Sat, 9 am—12 am. Restaurant hours vary. Reservations recommended.

COST
➤ Elevator: Adults $11, seniors (over 64) $9, children (5 to 12) $5, under 5 free. Elevator charge is waived for guests who eat at the restaurant and spend $15 each for lunch or $25 each for dinner (excluding alcohol).

GETTING THERE
➤ By car from I-5, take one of the Seattle Center Exits and follow the signs. Some free parking is available on nearby streets. During special

events, parking fees at Center parking lots are based on the number of people in the vehicle (discounts for 2 or more). Expect to pay from $6 to $12 for all-day parking. About 5 minutes from downtown Seattle.
➤ By public transit, take any Metro bus from downtown headed north to Seattle Center. Call Metro Transit for route and schedule information (206) 553-3000.

NEARBY
➤ Downtown Seattle, Waterfront, Myrtle Edwards Park, Westlake Center, Monorail, Experience Music Project, Seattle Children's Theatre, Seattle Children's Museum.

COMMENT
➤ Plan a 1- to 1 1/2-hour visit without a restaurant stop.

A *Moving Feast*
SPIRIT OF WASHINGTON
DINNER TRAIN

625 S. 4th St., Renton
1-800-876-RAIL
www.spiritofwashingtondinertrain.com

Eastside residents have spotted this sleek red and silver dinner train gliding through their lakeside neighborhoods. Its classic elegance seems to say "expensive" and "just for grown-ups." It can however, be an enjoyable experience for families and at certain times of the year, it's a bargain too.

The three-hour train ride is definitely one of those outings where the trip is the attraction, at least for kids. Though it stops at Columbia Winery for about 45 minutes, children may not enjoy touring the winery or wandering through the upscale gift shop.

To pass the time there, explore the outside grounds and pose the kids alongside the train and the castle-like winery for photos.

As the train rolls past beautiful forests, meadows and waterfront homes, you'll be served first-class fare. The *Spirit of Washington Dinner Train* boasts delights such as crab crêpes and prime rib. Youngsters get their own menu of standard kid food, including hotdogs, pizza and cheeseburgers. On the way back, dessert is served—your choice of Chocolate Paradiso or a seasonal fruit specialty.

Since the entire ride is spent sitting at a dinner table, this may not be the best outing for an active preschooler. Bring coloring books, crayons or a deck of cards to keep little ones from growing fidgety. On evening trips, be sure to keep an eye out for the colorful hot air balloons above Woodinville.

SEASONS AND TIMES
➤ Year-round: Mon—Fri, 6:30 pm; Sat, noon and 6:30 pm; Sun, 11 am and 5:30 pm. (No trips on Mondays between October and May.)

COST
➤ Dinner: Adults $60, under 13 $20. Lunch: Adults $50, under 13 $20. Dome seating is $10 extra. Between November and April, up to 2 children (under 13) ride and eat free per paying adult.

GETTING THERE
➤ By car, from Seattle center, head east on Mercer St. to I-5 South. Take I-5 S. to the I-405 N. (Renton) Exit. Take Exit 2 (167 Renton/Rainier Ave.) from I-405 and continue north on Rainier Ave. S. Turn east on S. 3rd St., then south on Burnett Ave. S. to the Train Depot. Free parking. About 35 minutes from Seattle Center.

Roll Back in Time
SNOQUALMIE VALLEY RAILROAD

38625 S.E. King St., Snoqualmie
(425) 888-3030
www.trainmuseum.org

L
ess than an hour from the city, step back in time on the Snoqualmie Valley Railroad. Pulled by a diesel locomotive, the *Cascade Foothills Limited* consists of restored passenger cars built in 1912 and 1915. It's a great way to introduce young kids to train travel. The ride is short, and passengers are welcome to walk around the train and explore. In good weather, sitting in the open-windowed car is especially fun.

The train meanders along a five-mile route, through meadows and forest, over a river, past modest country homes and farms and into the small towns of Snoqualmie and North Bend. When you arrive at either end, you can quickly stretch your legs and hop back on, or stay longer for lunch and explore the town's shops. Your tickets are valid to catch a later train back, just don't miss the last one! Trains depart from the Snoqualmie station on the hour and from the North Bend station on the half hour.

For a special treat, head to the North Bend Depot to ride the *Santa Train* in December. This holiday excursion includes refreshments served in a railway kitchen car (hot chocolate with cookies baked in coal-burning stoves), a visit with Santa Claus and a small gift. To protect passengers from cold weather, all of the railway cars have glass windows in winter. After the train ride, families can purchase their Christmas tree—several tree farms are nearby in the upper Snoqualmie Valley. Year-round, the Northwest Railway Museum (page 195) is open at the Snoqualmie Depot. A small bookstore sells "all things train."

SEASONS AND TIMES

➺ Train rides: Apr—May, Sun, 11 am—4 pm; Memorial Day—Oct, Sat—Sun, 11 am—4 pm. *Santa Train:* First three weekends in Dec, 9 am—3 pm (hourly). Northwest Railway Museum: Memorial Day—Sept, daily, 11 am—7 pm; Oct—Memorial Day, Thu—Mon, 10 am—5 pm.

COST

➺ Train rides: Adults $7, seniors (over 61) $6, children (3 to 12) $5, under 3 free. *Santa Train:* Individuals $9, under 3 free (advance ticket purchase required).

GETTING THERE

➺ By car, from Seattle Center, take Mercer St. east to I-5 South. Take I-5 S. to the I-90 E. Exit and proceed on I-90 to Exit 27. Follow the signs to downtown Snoqualmie. The Snoqualmie Depot is at the south side of the intersection of King St. and Railroad Ave. To get to the North Bend Depot, take Exit 31 from I-90 and turn north onto Hwy. 202, heading into North Bend. Turn west on North Bend Way. Go 2 blocks and park on the street; depot is at 205 McClellan St. About 40 minutes from Seattle Center.

NEARBY

➺ Snoqualmie Falls, North Bend, Issaquah.

COMMENT

➺ Plan a minimum 1 1/2 hour visit for round-trip ride and walking through the museum. Tickets for the *Santa Train* go on sale in mid-September and sell out quickly.

Navigating Puget Sound
WASHINGTON STATE FERRIES

**Seattle Waterfront Terminal, West Seattle/Fauntleroy
Terminal, Edmonds Terminal, Seattle
1-800-84-FERRY
www.wsdot.wa.gov/ferries/**

Where can you run around on a big ship deck, get blown around by cool sea breezes, play video race car games, watch tankers pass and toss popcorn to seagulls hovering off the port side, all for a walk-on fare of under $4? The answer is a Washington State Ferry.

Not only is ferrying inexpensive, it's educational. No matter what ship you take (Washington's ferry system has 27 boats, 20 terminals and 10 routes), it is likely you will see ocean life—everything from whales to scavenger birds. Ferries usually carry large maps of Puget Sound, historical photos and displays of local artisans and photographers. Most large ships also feature easy-to-read historical displays.

For a quick trip across the Sound, ride the ferry from downtown Seattle to Bainbridge. Bring your car and drive to Poulsbo on the other side. Kids love this quaint theme town that has several shops and a popular bakery with mouth-watering baked goods. For a short introductory ride to ferrying, try the 15-minute crossing from West Seattle to Vashon. Bring a picnic lunch and a soccer ball and make a day of it by visiting the island parks. Stop by the Chamber of Commerce (206-463-6217) to pick up a map of the area.

One of the busiest routes, Edmonds to Kingston, is perfect for a morning jaunt. Have an ice-cream cone and lounge on the dockside beach in Kingston before making the return trip. Ride the ferry to Bremerton and visit the waterfront park, marina and historic Puget Sound Naval Shipyard. Whatever route you choose, taking the ferry is one of Seattle's unique and cheap travel treats.

SEASONS AND TIMES
➤ Ferry schedules are produced quarterly. Pick one up on any state ferry or visit ferry travel expert Dan Youra's website *The On Line Ferry Travel Guide* at www.youra.com/ferry/

COST
➤ Varies. Generally between $1.15 (discounted walk-on from Seattle to Vashon) to $35.55 (round-trip vehicle and driver to Sidney, B.C. from Anacortes). Children under 5 ride free. Cash, in-state checks and traveler's checks are accepted, but credit cards are not. Discounts for youth passes, seniors and disabled people.

GETTING THERE
➤ By car, from Seattle Center, head west on Broad St. towards Puget Sound. Turn south on Alaskan Way and continue to the Alaskan Way Viaduct and park. About 10 minutes from Seattle center.
➤ By public transit, walk from Seattle Center to the Waterfront Street Car Route 99 and ride it to the Viaduct. Call Metro Transit for route and schedule information (206) 553-3000.

NEARBY
➤ Downtown Seattle, The Waterfront, Pike Place Market; near Fauntleroy in West Seattle is Lincoln Park; in Edmonds there are several beaches.

COMMENT

➤ Avoid rush hour (weekdays, 7 to 8 am and 4 to 6 pm). Birthday parties are welcome. Not all ferries are accessible to the disabled. Diaper changing stations available.

Other Ways To See Seattle

Gray Line of Seattle

800 Convention Place, Seattle
(206) 624-5077 or 1-800-426-7505
www.graylineofseattle.com

Tour the city without driving in traffic. Several excusions are offered, ranging from three-hour tours of the city (starting at $27 for adults and $13 for children) to day trips of Mount Rainier or Victoria, B.C. Gray Line also operates the Seattle Trolley bus. One ticket (adults $16, children under 13 $8) gets you on and off the trolley at any of its stops, on the day of purchase and the following day. The trolley stops at one of 11 tourist-friendly locations every 30 minutes, so it's easy to explore the city at your own pace while still enjoying the benefit of a narrated tour. Buy tickets at the Convention Center, Planet Hollywood kiosk (1500 – 6th Ave.), or at the front desk of many downtown hotels.

➤ Summer: Daily, 10 am—8 pm. Winter: Daily, 9 am—6 pm.

Sightseeing of Seattle
(206) 526-1444

This company offers a four-and-a-half-hour afternoon city tour for $40 (including beverage and pastry at a coffee shop stop) and a two-hour morning tour for $23. Narrated tours are aboard luxury mini-coaches and include all the best-known tourist attractions, as well as a close look at Seattle neighborhoods. Complimentary pick-up and drop-off at local hotels is provided; reservations required.

Casual Cab Co.
Waterfront (Alaskan Way)
and Pioneer Square area, Seattle
(206) 623-2991

For environmentally friendly transportation, it doesn't get much better than a pedicab, especially since you can relax and enjoy the ride and have someone else do the pedaling. Find pedicabs along Alaskan Way in Seattle's Waterfront area and in the Pioneer Square district. Fares are negotiated with the driver.

Emerald City Charters
Pier 54, Seattle
(206) 624-3931 or 1-800-831-3274

Experience Puget Sound by water on a 90-minute sailboat ride for $23 per person. Three departures are available daily between May 1 and October 15. A two-and-a-half-hour sunset sail costs $38.

Over the Rainbow Balloon Flights
Woodinville
(425) 861-8611 or (206) 364-0995

Northeast of downtown Seattle, the early evening skies over the Sammamish Valley (western Washington's wine country) are often dotted by colorful hot air balloons. It's an expensive adventure ($165 per person), but if you've got the money and want to celebrate a special event in a unique way, then "the sky's the limit."

Argosy Cruises
Seattle Waterfront (Piers 55 and 57), Lake Union (AGC Marina), and Kirkland (Marina Park), Seattle
(206) 623-1445 or 1-800-642-7816
www.argosycruises.com

Cruise Lake Washington, Lake Union or Harbor. Argosy's two-hour trips are a great way to view the city from the water and get the scoop on some of the city's popular curiosity points. The rides are great for school-aged children, but tots tend to lose interest quickly. If you have particularly well-mannered children, consider the Royal Argosy Dinner Cruise.

➤ Year-round: Daily. Call for a complete list of departure times. Costs vary depending on trip. Adults between $16 and $30, children (4 to 12) between $10 and $16.

CHAPTER 11

FAVORITE FESTIVALS

Introduction

When it comes to festivals, Seattle is one happening place. If you're visiting in the summer, you won't want to miss Seattle's month-long Seafair—rated the 10th most popular festival in the U.S. Still going strong after more than half a century, it includes dozens of community fairs, parades, hydroplane races, air shows, ship tours and other special events.

The free Folklife Festival is held over Memorial Day weekend and offers families music, dance and other cultural events. Want to sample tasty treats? Don't miss Bite of Seattle. It serves up affordable fare from noted local restaurants, free samples from food vendors, live entertainment and an interactive area for kids. The Seattle International Children's Festival highlights performances from around the world, and Bumbershoot features thousands of artists sharing their talents in music, dance, theater, comedy and more.

Seattle Center produces several of its own festivals for families, including Whirligig, Winterfest and a series of 13 ethnic festivals called Festál. In this chapter you can also learn about WOMAD USA, a music and arts festival in East King County, the Puyallup Fair and Camlann Medieval Faire. For some holiday delights, head to Downtown December for a visit to the Teddy Bear Suite and a ride on the Holiday Carousel. Look for other festivals and special events included in the Directory of Events at the back of this book.

Taste of the Town
BITE OF SEATTLE

Seattle Center, Seattle
(206) 232-2982
www.biteofseattle.com

This annual food frenzy features some of the city's best restaurants serving up tasty treats at affordable prices. More than 100 booths are set up at the Seattle Center grounds—60 are restaurateurs with the remainder being food product vendors. Vendors often have free samples including beverages and snacks. Every restaurant offers at least one two-dollar item, so you can enjoy a delectable or two while paying bargain prices. But be warned: the scents of familiar and exotic foods will make it difficult to control your palate. If temptation gets the better of your family, splurge on "the Alley" special—it includes items from eight restaurants for eight dollars per person.

There's plenty of fun to be had while feasting, as live entertainment plays on five outdoor stages throughout the weekend. The special Kids' Zone serves up interactive games, contests and performances by top local children's entertainers. There's even an inflatable bouncing area for your kids to burn off steam.

The Bite is one of Seattle's bigger festivals with crowds to match. Consider taking the bus (shuttles run from several Park and Rides), riding the Monorail from downtown or carpooling. It's a good idea to pick a meeting spot beforehand in the event your kids get separated. Try to visit on Friday or in the morning when crowds are smaller.

SEASONS AND TIMES
→ Mid-July: Fri—Sat, 11 am—9 pm; Sun, 11 am—8 pm. Usually the third weekend in July.

COST
→ Free admission to festival. Restaurants offer $2 tastes and meals up to $6.

GETTING THERE
→ By car, from I-5, take the Mercer St. Exit and head west towards the Space Needle. Some free parking is available on nearby streets. During special events, parking fees at Center parking lots are based on number of people in vehicle (discounts for two or more). Expect to pay from $6 to $12 for all-day parking.
→ By public transit, more than a dozen Metro bus routes service Seattle Center. Festival shuttles run from several suburban Park and Ride lots during special events. Call Metro Transit for route and schedule information (206) 553-3000. Or, ride the monorail that travels between Seattle Center and downtown Seattle's Westlake Center.

NEARBY
→ Downtown Seattle, Waterfront, Pike Place Market, Pacific Science Center, Seattle Children's Theatre, Space Needle, Experience Music Project, Children's Museum.

COMMENT
→ Plan a 2- to 3-hour visit. It's generally too crowded to use a stroller. Proceeds from "the Alley" go to hunger charities.

Arts Umbrella
BUMBERSHOOT

Seattle Center, Seattle
(206) 281-8111
www.bumbershoot.org

For Seattle-area families, Labor Day weekend means more than just the end of summer vacation. It's time for Bumbershoot—Seattle's famed four-day arts festival. Featuring thousands of artists on more than two dozen indoor and outdoor stages, Bumbershoot offers something for the whole family.

Want to catch a movie, see paintings or sculptures, watch acrobats in action or hear poetry? Since 1971, Bumbershoot has been offering these and other activities to residents and tourists alike. Youngsters shouldn't miss the Kids Hands-On Arts and Literary Arts Program. Feel the beat as one of the many musical talents graces a Bumbershoot stage. In the past, the festival has hosted such famed performers as Gladys Knight, Macy Gray, Tina Turner, Bonnie Raitt and Ladysmith Black Mambazo. There's also a book fair, Visual Arts exhibits, a film festival and plenty of children's entertainment.

Bumbershoot's one-day pass is good for all venues. There's plenty of food on-site but if you want to cut costs, pack a lunch and people-watch while you munch. Pick a site to meet in the event your family gets separated—it's very crowded.

SEASONS AND TIMES
➤ Labor Day weekend: Fri–Mon, 11 am–10 pm.

COST
➤ One-day pass: Adults $10 (in advance) $14 (at the gate), under 13 free. Prices subject to change. Call ahead to confirm.

GETTING THERE
➤ By car, from I-5, take the Mercer St. Exit and head west towards the Space Needle. Some free parking is available on nearby streets. During special events, parking fees at Center parking lots are based on number of people in vehicle (discounts for two or more). Expect to pay from $6 to $12 for all-day parking.
➤ By public transit, more than a dozen Metro bus routes service Seattle Center. Festival shuttles run from several suburban Park and Ride lots during special events. Call Metro Transit for route and schedule information (206) 553-3000. Or, ride the monorail that travels between Seattle Center and downtown Seattle's Westlake Center.

NEARBY
➤ Downtown Seattle, Waterfront, Pike Place Market, Pacific Science Center, Seattle Children's Theatre, Space Needle, Experience Music Project, Children's Museum.

COMMENT
➤ Be sure to look for the Bumbershoot schedule in the city newspapers the week before Labor Day weekend. Prepare a schedule for the festival. Plan to spend several hours a day for at least two days.

Knights, Minstrels and More
CAMLANN MEDIEVAL FAIRE

10320 Kelley Rd. N.E., Carnation
(425) 788-8624
www.camlann.com

Hearken back to an age when chivalry was the rule and village life was simple. Visit Camlann Medieval Village, an hour's drive from Seattle in the tiny town of Carnation. Throughout the year, the village hosts numerous colorful feasts and special events, such as St. George's Feast in April, a May Festival and an All Hallows Feast in October. The Camlann's Bors Hede Restaurant (open year-round) offers the Northwest's most unique dining experience, with food from medieval recipes accompanied by minstrel entertainment.

Participatory in nature, Camlann's special events are an invitation to dress up in medieval garb, work on your manners (greetings usually begin with 'milord' and 'milady') and join the fun. For those who would rather just quietly look and learn, Camlann Medieval Faire is a perfect introduction to life in the Middle Ages. The Faire is a seven-weekend event in July and August and is packed with demonstrations by artisans, shows featuring knights in combat, strolling minstrels, artists and story-tellers. Don't miss The Camlann HandCraft Shop, featuring all manner of medieval art, craft and clothing. Brush up on your medieval English by visiting Scribes Shop, a bookstore specializing in tomes about the Middle Ages.

The Medieval Faire is a unique experience that your kids are bound to enjoy. Head your horse, er, car east to Camlann Village and return to a more colorful, self-sufficient time in history.

SEASONS AND TIMES
➙ Mid-July—late Aug: Sat—Sun, 11:3o am—6 pm.

COST
➤ Adults $8, children (6 to 12) $5, under 6 free. Prices subject to change so call to confirm.

GETTING THERE
➤ By car, from Seattle Center, head east on Mercer St. to I-5 North. Take I-5 N. to the SR- 520 Exit (Bellevue). Follow SR-520 until it ends and becomes Avondale Rd. Turn north on Avondale for 1 mile, then head east onto Novelty Hill Rd. for about 5 miles. Turn north onto East Snoqualmie Valley Rd. then head east onto 124th Ave. Cross the valley and turn south on SR-203. Continue south for 4 miles and turn east onto Stillwater Hill Rd. Signs to Camlann Medieval Village will appear in about 1 mile. About 1 hour from Seattle Center.

COMMENT
➤ Plan to visit for half a day or more. Stick around for a meal at the restaurant. It is tasty and unique.

Holiday Delights
DOWNTOWN IN DECEMBER

**Throughout Downtown Seattle
(206) 623-0340 (Downtown Seattle Association)
www.downtownseattle.com**

The holiday season kicks off the Friday morning after Thanksgiving with the Bon Marché's Holiday Parade. It features floats and characters covered with colorful balloons. When the parade ends, the Holiday Carousel at Westlake Park gets going, with daily rides through to New Year's Eve (closed on Christmas). In the evening, crowds gather to hear live holiday music as more than 10,000 lights on the towering tree in Westlake Center are officially lit. Then, the legendary Bon Marché Holiday Star lights up and a fireworks show heralds the festive season.

Throughout the month of December, downtown Seattle is filled with festive delights—carolers, live music performances, the smell of roasting chestnuts and special displays in store windows and hotels. Bring your kids to meet Santa in the Bon Marché's special Santa shop, at Westlake Center or at Nordstrom. Stroll along the streets and ogle the horse-drawn carriages touring blanket-covered riders.

Families will want to put two attractions at the top of their list. The Teddy Bear Suite at the Four Seasons Olympic Hotel (411 University St.; 206-287-4001) is filled to the brim with teddy bears, books about teddy bears and free teddy bear-shaped cookies. Don't forget your camera so you can pose your youngsters among the charming bears. A few blocks away, the Sheraton Seattle (6th and Pike; 206-447-5547) hosts a fanciful Gingerbread Village. Kids and grown-ups marvel at the creations of local architectural firms who worked in partnership with the Sheraton's chefs to design and build the eight structures made of gingerbread. Visitors' donations benefit the Juvenile Diabetes Foundation.

SEASONS AND TIMES
➤ Most activities: The day after Thanksgiving—New Year's. Teddy Bear Suite: The day after Thanksgiving—Dec 24. Gingerbread Village: The day after Thanksgiving—Dec 26.

COST
➤ Free. $1 donation to ride carousel. A small fee may apply to other activities.

GETTING THERE

➤ By car, from Seattle Center, take 5th Ave. south about 8 blocks and park along the street at meters or park in a pay lot ($5 to $10). About 3 minutes from Seattle Center.

➤ By public transit, ride the 3-minute Monorail to Westlake Center. Or walk along 5th Ave. It's a 20-minute walk.

Twelve Months of Fun
FESTIVALS FOR
ALL SEASONS

Seattle Center, Seattle
(206) 684-7200
www.seattlecenter.com

Besides playing host to a variety of festivals, Seattle Center produces many of its own seasonal family events. The kids' favorite is definitely Whirligig, an indoor spring carnival that will keep your children busy. With inflatable rides, hands-on arts and crafts, games, plenty of free music and drama performances, the festival is geared specifically to those aged ten and under.

If you're looking for a little holiday cheer, Winterfest is the place for you. From the day after Thanksgiving until New Year's, Seattle Center is decorated with twinkling lights and filled with the sounds of the season, from carolers to musicians to children's entertainers. You can shop for unique items at the Winterfest World Market and be mesmerized by the holiday train display. Beginner and expert skaters will be enticed to take a whirl in the open air at the outdoor ice rink. Other festivities include the celebration of Kwanzaa, the Chinese New

Year and the Asian Pacific Holiday Celebration. There's also a free Hanukkah show and a huge fireworks display launched from the Space Needle to ring in the New Year.

To learn about the diverse ethnic heritage of the region, Seattle Center offers families a series of 13 cultural festivals called Festál. From the African-American Festival to the Japanese Cherry Blossom Festival to celebrating the Hmong New Year in November, your family can't go wrong with these entertaining, educational experiences.

Be sure to call ahead for specific dates and times. Stop the by information desk at the Center House to get a brochure of upcoming events or visit Seattle Center's website.

SEASONS AND TIMES
➤ Whirligig: Mar—Apr, Sun—Thu, 11 am—4 pm; Fri—Sat, 11 am—6 pm. Winterfest: Friday after Thanksgiving—New Year's, hours vary. Call or visit website for schedule. Festál: Jan—Nov. Call for specific dates and times.

COST
➤ Free. Fees apply for Whirligig rides, Winterfest Ice Rink, some dances and special shows at festivals.

GETTING THERE
➤ By car, from I-5, take the Mercer St. Exit and head west towards the Space Needle. Some free parking is available on nearby streets. During special events, parking fees at Center parking lots are based on number of people in vehicle (discounts for two or more). Expect to pay from $6 to $12 for all-day parking.
➤ By public transit, more than a dozen Metro bus routes service Seattle Center. Festival shuttles run from several suburban park & ride lots during special events, Or, ride the monorail that travels between Seattle Center and downtown Seattle's Westlake Center. Call Metro Transit for route and schedule information (206) 553-3000.

NEARBY
➤ Downtown Seattle, Waterfront, Pike Place Market, Pacific Science Center, Seattle Children's Theatre, Space Needle, Experience Music Project, Children's Museum.

COMMENT
➤ You can spend an hour or a day, depending on the event.

Folk Art at
NORTHWEST FOLKLIFE
FESTIVAL

Seattle Center, Seattle
(206) 684-7300
www.nwfolklife.org

I f you want to show your kids a little culture, visit one of Seattle's oldest and largest festivals, the Northwest Folklife Festival. Each Memorial Day weekend, Folklife becomes home to thousands of regional and international folk artists. They share their cultural and family traditions through music and dance performances, workshops, exhibits, demonstrations and films. The best part is that everything's free!

The Folklife Festival is one big music jam session, so bring your instruments and wander around. On just about every corner and grassy knoll you'll find a pick-up group happy to have you join in. Folklife also offers plenty just for kids—wandering around Seattle Center, they will be dazzled by puppeteers, jugglers and other children's entertainers. There are hand-on arts and crafts to do and plenty of fun foods (elephant ears, ethnic foods, strawberry shortcake to name a few) to snack on.

While there, be sure to stop and buy your Folklife button. The buttons are usually sold for a couple of dollars and are the festival's main source of funding— a reasonable price for four days of incredible entertainment.

SEASONS AND TIMES
➤ Memorial Day weekend: Fri—Mon, 11 am—11 pm.

COST
➤ Free.

GETTING THERE
➤ By car, from I-5, take the Mercer St. Exit and head west towards the Space Needle. Some free parking is available on nearby streets. During special events, parking fees at Center parking lots are based on number of people in vehicle (discounts for two or more). Expect to pay from $6 to $12 for all-day parking.
➤ By public transit, more than a dozen Metro bus routes service Seattle Center. Festival shuttles run from several suburban park & ride lots during special events. Or, ride the monorail that travels between Seattle Center and downtown Seattle's Westlake Center. Call Metro Transit for route and schedule information (206) 553-3000.

NEARBY
➤ Downtown Seattle, Waterfront, Pike Place Market, Pacific Science Center, Seattle Children's Theatre, Space Needle, Experience Music Project, Children's Museum.

COMMENT
➤ Be sure to look for the Northwest Folklife Festival schedule in the city newspapers the week before Memorial Day weekend. Prepare a schedule for the festival. Plan to spend several hours a day for at least two days.

Moooooove Over Summer!
THE PUYALLUP FAIR

110 – 9th Ave. S.W., Puyallup
(253) 841-5045
www.thefair.com

Do you have an aspiring young farmer or vet in your midst? Then saddle up and head over to the Puyallup—one of the largest fairs of its kind in the nation. The sprawling 160-acre grounds may seem daunting to youngsters, so be sure to pick up a map at the entrance. Let your kids pick out the activities they want to visit most and then start exploring.

For farm fun, check out the pig races, dairy demonstrations, the Kids' Pioneer Farm Planting Patch and the 4-H and Future Farmers of America animals and exhibits. Nuzzle furry friends at the Petting Farm, or watch magnificent draft horse demonstrations in the arena. If your family prefers arts and crafts, take in egg artistry, glass blowing, weaving or spinning demonstrations. You can even watch a blacksmith in action or attend a Mad Science Show.

And there's more. Like any good fair, the Puyallup has rides galore—a giant Ferris wheel, the Spider ride, and a kid-ride area with tamer rides for toddlers. A video arcade will entice older kids. There are also clowns, jugglers and other performers on the premises. The lines for the rides are often long and the area is very crowded. Be sure to establish a meeting place in the event your family gets separated. With so much to see, it's likely that one day won't be enough for your children. To make it more enjoyable, pick specific events to attend and visit the fair several times for a few hours.

SEASONS AND TIMES
➤ Three weeks in Sept: Mon—Thu, 8 am—10 pm; Fri—Sat, 10 am—11 pm; Sun, 10 am—10 pm. Call for exact dates.

COST
➤ Adults $7.50, seniors (over 61) and children (6 to 18) $4.50, under 6 free. Prices may be subject to change so call ahead to confirm.

GETTING THERE
➤ By car, from Seattle Center, go east on Mercer St. to I-5 South. Take the I-405 N. Exit off I-5 S. and head east towards Renton. Take the SR-167 (Valley Freeway) Exit heading south towards Renton/Auburn. Then take SR-512 W. heading southeast toward Puyallup. Take the Meridian St. S. Exit and turn south. Turn east on 9th Ave. S.W. Signs to the Puyallup Fairgrounds are clearly marked on all highways—keep on the lookout for the emerald green and white markers. Parking is available in lots or on the lawns of fairground neighbors ($5 to $20). About 45 minutes from Seattle Center.
➤ By public transit (via Metro with connection to Pierce Transit), call Metro Transit for route and schedule information (206) 553-3000 or Pierce Transit 800-562-8109.

COMMENT
➤ Wheelchair rentals available.

Summer Celebrations
SEAFAIR

Throughout Greater Seattle
(206) 728-0123
www.seafair.com

Since 1950, the Seattle area has celebrated summer in style with a month-long extravaganza known as Seafair. One of the largest festivals in the U.S., Seafair boasts parades, air shows, hydroplane races and dozens of free community events. Some of the highlights are the Milk Carton Derby at Green Lake (teams race water-borne vehicles made of milk cartons), the Torchlight Parade, the Fleet Arrival and ship tours, and an air show featuring the world-famous Blue Angels.

Festivals and fairs are held in many of the city's neighborhoods as well as in nearby towns, including the Chinatown-International District Summer Festival, Redmond Derby Days, Renton River Days, Kent Cornucopia Days, Des Moines Waterland Festival and others. Numerous parades take to the streets, including two just for kids (Wallingford Kiddie Parade and University District Junior Parade). Check the Seafair website and local newspapers for a complete schedule of events.

SEASONS AND TIMES
➤ Early July–late Aug. Some community events may occur later in the year.

COST
➤ Free admission to parades and festivals. Fees for reserved seating at hydro races.

GETTING THERE
➤ For information on getting to Seafair events, call the Seafair office or visit Seafair's website.

Just for Kids
SEATTLE INTERNATIONAL CHILDREN'S FESTIVAL

**Seattle Center, 158 Thomas St., Seattle
(206) 684-7336
www.seattleinternational.org**

The Seattle International Children's Festival is "the thing" for families to do in May. Performers from around the globe spend six days putting on artistic shows in a variety of languages, from English to Japanese to Spanish. Watch a puppet show, a musical chef or a hip-hop circus. Although the shows change each year, you can count on high quality entertainment that will have the family asking for more.

The Festival has a plethora of hands-on discovery centers where children and adults can make great art, learn about various cultures, fish for prizes or design their own kites. Be sure to stop in at the World of Games center where a roomful of traditional board games from around the world await your family. Check in at the Healthy Habitat where activities and demonstrations educate youngsters about the global implications of a healthy environment.

School groups can really get their money's worth, too. There are teacher packages available, as well as reduced prices for student admission. Call or visit the website for details. No matter how old you or your kids are, the Seattle International Children's Festival offers a world of knowledge and fun in one place.

SEASONS AND TIMES
➤ Mid-May. Shows: Mon—Fri, 10 am, 10:15 am, 11:30 am, 11:45 am and 1 pm. Additional shows on Thu—Sat, call for details. Discovery Centers: Mon—Wed, 9:30 am—2:30 pm; Thu—Fri, 9:30 am—7 pm; Sat, 9 am—5 pm.

COST
➤ Prices vary. Expect to pay about $8 per show. Special prices for schools and other groups.

GETTING THERE
➤ By car, from I-5, take the Mercer St. Exit and head west towards the Space Needle. Some free parking is available on nearby streets. During special events, parking fees at Center parking lots are based on number of people in vehicle (discounts for two or more). Expect to pay from $6 to $12 for all-day parking.
➤ By public transit, more than a dozen Metro bus routes service Seattle Center. Festival shuttles run from several suburban park & ride lots during special events. Or, ride the monorail that travels between Seattle Center and downtown Seattle's Westlake Center. Call Metro Transit for route and schedule information (206) 553-3000.

NEARBY
➤ Downtown Seattle, Waterfront, Pike Place Market, Pacific Science Center, Seattle Children's Theatre, Space Needle, Experience Music Project, Children's Museum.

COMMENT
→ Be sure to look for the International Children's Festival schedule in the city newspapers and parenting publications in early May. Plan several hours each visit.

Musical Melodies at
WOMAD USA

Marymoor Park
6046 W. Lake Sammamish Pkwy. N.E., Redmond
(206) 281-8111
www.womadusa.com

A re your kids movers and shakers? Then mark the World Music Arts and Dance U.S.A. Festival (WOMAD) down on your calendar. This three-day extravaganza celebrates the passion and artistry of cultures from around the world, bringing dozens of spectacular performers together in a spacious outdoor setting.

WOMAD artists offer hands-on workshops in their craft. The large kids' activity area invites youngsters to make instruments, traditional masks and other cultural symbols. They'll learn about music, dance and art perfected by festival performers through lectures and small workshops.

There's food available on-site, as well as a global market when you can purchase ethnic crafts, musical instruments, jewelry and more. Although admission fees may deter some families, the experience is well worth the cost, especially since children under 12 are free. Essentially, this festival is a fabulous way to introduce your children to a wide variety of international music. Don't be surprised if they're not the only ones dancing to the beat.

SEASONS AND TIMES
➤ Late July for 3 days. Visit website or call for dates and times.

COST
➤ Adult Day Pass $35, under 12 free when accompanied by adult. Price subject to change so call ahead to confirm.

GETTING THERE
➤ By car, from Seattle Center, head east on Mercer St. to I-5 North. Take I-5 N. and get off at the SR-520 Exit (Bellevue). Follow SR-520 and exit at West Lake Sammamish Parkway N.E. Head south at the stoplight. Turn east into Marymoor Park. Parking in Marymoor Park's parking lot. About 40 minutes from Seattle Center.
➤ By public transit, Metro shuttle available from downtown Seattle and Northgate Mall Park & Ride station in North Seattle. Call Metro within 1 month prior to event for shuttle schedule information at (206) 553-3000.

COMMENT
➤ Plan to visit for at least half a day.

Room & Board

KID-FRIENDLY
RESTAURANTS

E ating out with the family offers numerous rewards, chief among them is that someone else does the cooking. Luckily, plenty of restaurants around Seattle offer families a fun atmosphere, good food and reasonable prices. Better still, the staff is friendly and most provide kids' menus or kid-sized portions upon request, booster and high chairs and crayons and paper to keep little hands occupied. Many accommodate nursing moms and have baby changing stations.

Some of Seattle's most popular family-style restaurants are listed below. If you want to introduce your kids to ethnic delectables, visit some of Seattle's neighborhoods. You'll find excellent Chinese food in the International District and delicious Indian fare in the University District. For Scandinavian cuisine, Ballard is the spot and African and African American specialties can be found in Capitol Hill. For more information on Seattle's dining scene, check out *Best Places (Seattle)* and *Seattle Cheap Eats* published by Sasquatch Press (206) 467-4300 or www. sasquatchbooks.com. Or, go online to www. seattle.citysearch.com/section/restaurants.

Great Breakfast Joints

Mr. Bills
(1950s-style diner with memorabilia; greasy spoon fare; kids' menu; inexpensive)
930 N. 130th St., Seattle (206) 362-7777

Luna Park Café
(Funky memorabilia; great American fare; large servings; kids' menu)
2918 S.W. Avalon Way, Seattle (206) 935-7250

Mae's Phinney Ridge Café
(Breakfast served all day; kids' menu; excellent potatoes, coffeecake and milkshakes)
6412 Phinney Ave. N., Seattle (206) 782-1222

Patty's Eggnest
(Kids' menu; home-style cooking; aquarium filled with fish)
2202 N. 45th St., Seattle (206) 675-0645

Favorite Eateries for Families of All Sizes

Red Robin
(Huge kids' menu; great burgers and shakes; birthday parties)
1101 Alaskan Way, Seattle (206) 623-1942
1100 4th Ave., Seattle (206) 447-1909
3272 Fuhrman Ave. E., Seattle (206) 323-0918
555 Northgate Plaza, Suite 430, Seattle (206) 365-0933

Diggity Dog Hot Dogs and Sausages
(Wide variety of hotdogs; photos, art and kitsch)
5421 Meridian Ave. N., Seattle (206) 633-1966

Dick's Drive Ins

(A Seattle institution since the 1950s; great fries, burgers, milkshakes)
115 Broadway E., Seattle (206) 323-1300
9208 Holman Rd. N.W., Seattle (206) 783-5233
500 Queen Anne Ave. N., Seattle (206) 285-5155
12325 - 30th N.E., Seattle (206) 363-7777
111 N.E. 45th St., Seattle (206) 632-5125

Kidd Valley Hamburger Co.

(A must with kids; great burgers, fries, fried mushrooms; kids meals come in a paper car)
4910 Green Lake Way N., Seattle (206) 547-0121
5502 - 25th N.E., Seattle (206) 522-0890
135 - 15th E., Seattle (206) 328-8133
418 Northgate Mall, Seattle (206) 306-9516
531 Queen Anne N., Seattle (206) 284-0184
14303 Aurora Ave. N., Seattle (206) 364-8493

Yasuko's Teriyaki

(Fast service; take-out; food kids will eat)
4850 Green Lake Way N., Seattle (206) 675-8800
6850 Woodlawn Ave. N.E., Seattle (206) 527-0384
3200 - 15th Ave. W., Seattle (206) 283-9152
4402 - 35th St. S.W., Seattle (206) 932-3395
530 Broadway St., Seattle (206) 322-0123

Ivar's Fish Bars

(Fish 'n Chips; large servings)
1001 Alaskan Way, Suite 200, Seattle (206) 624-6852
401 N.E. Northlake Way, Seattle (206) 632-7223
6000 - 15th Ave. N.W., Seattle (206) 782-1602
3101 - 1st Ave., Seattle (206) 283-1575
467 Northgate Mall, Seattle (206) 367-4820
13448 Aurora Ave. N., Seattle (206) 365-2131

AGUA VERDE PADDLE CLUB

(Inexpensive; Mexican food; casual dining; take-out available; kayak rentals)
1303 N.E. Boat St., Seattle (206) 545-8570

Gravity Bar
(All vegetarian juice bar; futuristic décor; meals made
to order for finicky kids)
415 Broadway E., Seattle (206) 325-7186

Rositas
(colorful atmosphere; a penny fountain; big portions;
kids' menu; birthday parties)
7210 Woodlawn Ave. N.E., Seattle (206) 523-3031
9747 – 4th Ave. N.W., Seattle (206) 784-4132

Classy Dinner
and Kid-food Too

Cucina Cucina Italian Café
(Crayons and paper for drawing; festive atmosphere;
kids' menu; Italian fare; birthday parties)
901 Fairview Ave. N., Seattle (206) 447-2782

Buca di Beppos
(Movie star photos and memorabilia; Italian fare;
family-style service; huge portions)
701 – 9th Ave. N. Seattle (206) 244-2288

5 Spot
(Mason jar water glasses thrill kids; greasy spoon fare;
healthy alternatives; kids' menu; fun atmosphere)
1502 Queen Anne Ave. N., Seattle (206) 285-7768

Rainforest Café
(Jungle theme with mechanical animals, aquariums;
tropical environment; gift shop; kids' menu; birthdays;
great smoothies)
290 Southcenter Mall, Tukwila (206) 248-8882

Ivar's Salmon House
(Native American art decor; kids' menu comes on a paper
Native American mask; great for special occasions)
401 N.E. Northlake Way, Seattle (206) 632-0767

And for dessert . . .

Famous Pacific Desserts
(Delicious desserts of all varieties)
127 Mercer St., Seattle (206) 284-8100

Mix Ice Cream
(Create-your own ice cream masterpieces)
4507 University Way N.E., Seattle (206) 547-3436
4208 E. Madison St., Seattle (206) 324-0431

FAMILY-FRIENDLY HOTELS

L ooking for home-away-from-home comfort when you are on vacation? Staying at a hotel can be hectic when you're traveling as a family. New surroundings, an unfamiliar bed—it can unsettle even the most adventurous child. Whether your stay in Seattle is a couple of days or a couple of weeks, the family-friendly establishments below will help make sure your family wakes up refreshed and ready to take on a new day.

In addition to providing a relaxed atmosphere, most have services for families, from babysitting and kids' clubs to games rooms and more. These hotels are located in or near the downtown area and often offer seasonal discounts, weekend rates or other family specials. Visit www.supersaver.com for information about Seattle-area hotels' off-season Supersaver program.

Value

Seattle Inn
(Complimentary breakfast; indoor pool; playground; near Seattle Center)
225 Aurora Ave. N., Seattle (206) 728-7666 or (800) 255-7932
www.seattleinn.com

Moderate

Hampton Inn & Suites
(Complimentary breakfast; some rooms with kitchens)
700 – 5th Ave. N., Seattle (206) 282-7700 or (800)
HAMPTON (426-7866)

Homewood Suites
(Complimentary breakfast and afternoon snack; mini-grocery on site; suites with full kitchen)
206 Western Ave. W., Seattle (206) 281-9393 or (800) 225-5466

Inn at Harbor Steps
(Indoor pool; fireplaces; teddy bears; complimentary breakfast buffet and afternoon tea; cozy; in-room refrigerators)
1221 – 1st Ave., Seattle (206) 748-0973
www.foursisters.com/washington/index.html

Residence Inn
(Complimentary breakfast; indoor pool; kitchen; other locations in outlying areas of Seattle)
800 Fairview Ave. N., Seattle (206) 624-6000
www.residenceinn.com

Silver Cloud Inn
(Indoor and outdoor pool; complimentary shuttle to downtown; complimentary breakfast; laundry facilities)
Lake Union: 1150 Fairview Ave. N., Seattle (206) 447-9500
or (800) 330-5812 www.silvercloud.com
U-District: 5036 – 25th Ave. N.E. (206) 526-5200

Expensive

Four Seasons Olympic Hotel
(Excellent service; games and toys at concierge;
babysitting available; gifts and snacks for kids upon
arrival; indoor pool and health club)
411 University St., Seattle (206) 621-1700 or (800) 223-8772

Hotel Edgewater
(cozy lodge ambience; rubber ducky; waterfront
location)
Pier 67, 2411 Alaskan Way, Seattle (206) 728-7000
www.edgewaterhotel.com

Summerfield Suites by Wyndham
(Outdoor pool; suites with kitchen; complementary
breakfast)
1011 Pike St., Seattle (206) 682-8282 or (800) 833-4353
www.summerfieldsuites.com

Westin Seattle
(Kids' Club; gift pack; complimentary kids' beverages at
meals; infant safety kits; strollers; indoor pool)
1900 - 5th Ave., Seattle (206) 728-1000 or (800) 228-3000
www.westin.com

12 Months of Fun
DIRECTORY OF EVENTS

JANUARY
Mid-January
Martin Luther King Jr. Day
Celebration
Seattle Center
(206) 684-7200

Mid-January
Kids & Critters Naturefest
Northwest Trek Wildlife Park,
Eatonville
(800) 433-TREK (8735)

Late January
Têt Festival (Vietnamese New
Year)
Seattle Center
(206) 684-7200

FEBRUARY
Mid-February
Festival Sundiata (African-
American Festival)
Seattle Center
(206) 684-7200

Late February
Whirligig Preview
Seattle Center
(206) 684-7200

MARCH
Mid-March
Irish Heritage Week
Seattle Center
(206) 684-7200

Mid-March
St. Patrick's Day Parade
Downtown Seattle
(206) 623-0340

Mid-March
Purim Carnival
Stroum Jewish Community
Center, Mercer Island
(206) 232-7115

APRIL
Early April
Seattle Cherry Blossom and
Japanese Cultural Festival
Seattle Center
(206) 684-7200

Mid-April
Puyallup Spring Fair
Puyallup Fairgrounds, Puyallup
(253) 841-5045

Late-April
Daffodil Festival & Grand Floral
Street Parade
Downtown Tacoma
(253) 627-6176

MAY
Early May
Children's Day
Seattle Asian Art Museum
(206) 654-3100

Early May
Mom & Me at the Zoo
Woodland Park Zoo
(206) 506-4386

Mid-May
Maritime Week
Pier 48 through Pier 70
(206) 443-3830

Mid-May
University District Street Fair
University Way near University of
Washington
(206) 547-4417

Memorial Day Weekend
Pike Place Market Festival
Pike Place Market
(206) 587-0351

JUNE
Early June
Pagdiriwang Filipino Community
Festival
Seattle Center
(206) 684-7200

Early June
Pioneer Square Fire Festival
Pioneer Square district
(206) 622-6235

Mid-June
Chinese Culture and Arts Festival
Seattle Center
(206) 684-7200

Mid-June
Fremont District Street Fair &
Solstice Parade
Fremont neighborhood
(206) 547-7441

JULY
Independence Day
Fourth of Jul-Ivars
Myrtle Edwards Park
(206) 587-6500

Independence Day
Family Fourth Festival
Gas Works Park
(206) 281-8111

Early July
Chinatown/International District
Summer Festival
Hing Hay Park
(206) 728-0123

Mid-July
King County Fair
King County Fairgrounds,
Enumclaw
(206) 296-8888

Mid-July
Tivoli-Viking Days
Nordic Heritage Museum
(206) 789-5707

Late July
Bellevue Art Museum Fair
Bellevue Square, Bellevue
(425) 454-3322

Late July
Scottish Highland Games
King County Fairgrounds,
Enumclaw
(206) 522-2541

Late July
Central Area Community Festival
Garfield Community Center
(206) 684-4366

Late July
Ballard Seafoodfest
N.W. Market St.
(206) 784-9705

AUGUST
Mid-August
Bubble Festival
Pacific Science Center
(206) 443-2001

Mid-August
KOMO KidsFair
Seattle Center
(206) 404-4408

Late August
Canterbury Faire
Mill Creek Canyon Earthworks
Park, Kent
(253) 856-5050

Late August to Labor Day
Evergreen State Fair
Evergreen State Fairgrounds,
Monroe
(425) 339-3309

SEPTEMBER
Labor Day
Taste of Washington Farms
Pike Place Market
(206) 682-7453

Early September
Salmon Homecoming
Celebration
Seattle Aquarium and Waterfront
Park
(206) 386-4320

Early September
Tilth Organic Harvest Fair
Meridian Playground
(206) 633-0451

Early September
Greenspire Medieval Faire
Blessed Sacrament Church
(206) 732-8359

Mid-September
The Great Wallingford Wurst
Festival
St. Benedict School
(206) 632-3236

Mid-September
Fiestas Patrias
Seattle Center
(206) 684-7200

Late September
Fishermen's Fall Festival
Fishermen's Terminal
(206) 782-6577

Late September
Festa Italiana
Seattle Center
(206) 684-7200

OCTOBER
October
October Harvest Festival
Remlinger Farms, Carnation
(425) 451-8740

October
Pumpkin Country
Biringer Farm, Marysville
(425) 259-0255

Early October
Issaquah Salmon Days
Salmon hatchery & downtown
Issaquah
(206) 270-2532

Early October to mid-October
Molbak's Floral Fairyland
Molbak's Greenhouse and
Nursery, Woodinville
(425) 483-5000

Mid-October
Kelsey Creek Farm Fair
Kelsey Creek Farm, Bellevue
(425) 452-7688

Late October
Northwest Bookfest
Stadium Exhibition Center
(206) 378-1883

Late October
Trick-or-Treat on the Waterfront
Seattle Aquarium and Alaskan
Way businesses
(206) 386-4300

NOVEMBER
Early November
Hmong New Year Celebration
Seattle Center
(206) 684-7200

Mid-November
Yulefest
Nordic Heritage Museum
(206) 789-5707

Mid-November to late December
Festival of Lights
Children's Museum, Seattle
Center
(206) 441-1768

Thanksgiving Weekend
Model Railroad Show
Pacific Science Center
(206) 443-2001

**Late November to late
December**
Wells Fargo Ice Arena
Downtown Park, Bellevue
(425) 453-1223

**Late November to late
December**
Garden d'Lights
Bellevue Botanical Garden,
Bellevue
(425) 451-3755

**Late November to early
January**
Zoolights
Point Defiance Zoo & Aquarium,
Tacoma
(253) 591-5337

DECEMBER
Early December
SAM Lights Up!
Seattle Art Museum
(206) 654-3100

**Early December to mid-
December**
Christmas Ship Festival
Argosy Cruises
(206) 623-1445

**Early December to mid-
December**
Issaquah Reindeer Festival
Cougar Mountain Zoo, Issaquah
(425) 391-5508

Early or mid-December
Chanukah Celebration
Stroum Jewish Community
Center, Mercer Island
(206) 232-7115

Late December
Science Wonderland
Pacific Science Center
(206) 443-2001

Late December
Kwanzaa Celebration
Seattle Center
(206) 684-7200

Late December
Chinese New Year & Asian Pacific
Holiday Celebration
Seattle Center
(206) 684-7200

New Year's Eve Celebration
Seattle Center
(206) 684-7200

INDEX

THE LOBSTER KIDS' CITY EXPLORERS SERIES

$12.95 US · $17.95 CDN

The Lobster Kids' Guide to Exploring
BOSTON
By Deirdre Wilson
ISBN 1-894222-41-5

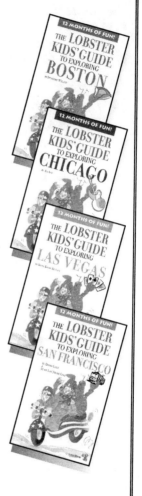

The Lobster Kids' Guide to Exploring
CHICAGO
By Ed Avis
ISBN 1-894222-40-7

The Lobster Kids' Guide to Exploring
LAS VEGAS
By Heidi Knapp Rinella
ISBN 1-894222-29-6

The Lobster Kids' Guide to Exploring
SAN FRANCISCO
By David Cole and Mary Lee Trees Cole
ISBN 1-894222-28-8

Available in all bookstores
or order from www.lobsterpress.com

THE LOBSTER KIDS' CITY EXPLORERS SERIES

$12.95 US • $17.95 CDN

The Lobster Kids' Guide to Exploring
CALGARY
By Kate Zimmerman with Diane Thuna
ISBN 1-894222-08-3

The Lobster Kids' Guide to Exploring
MONTRÉAL
By John Symon
Revised Edition
ISBN 1-894222-09-1

The Lobster Kids' Guide to Exploring
TORONTO
By Nathalie Ann Comeau
ISBN 1-894222-07-5

The Lobster Kids' Guide to Exploring
VANCOUVER
By Jeni Wright
ISBN 1-894222-05-9

The Lobster Kids' Guide to Exploring
OTTAWA-HULL
By John Symon
ISBN 1-894222-01-6
$12.95 US • $16.95 CDN

**Available in all bookstores
or order from www.lobsterpress.com**